COUNTER
RELIGIOUS

The Healing Power of Spiritual Friendships

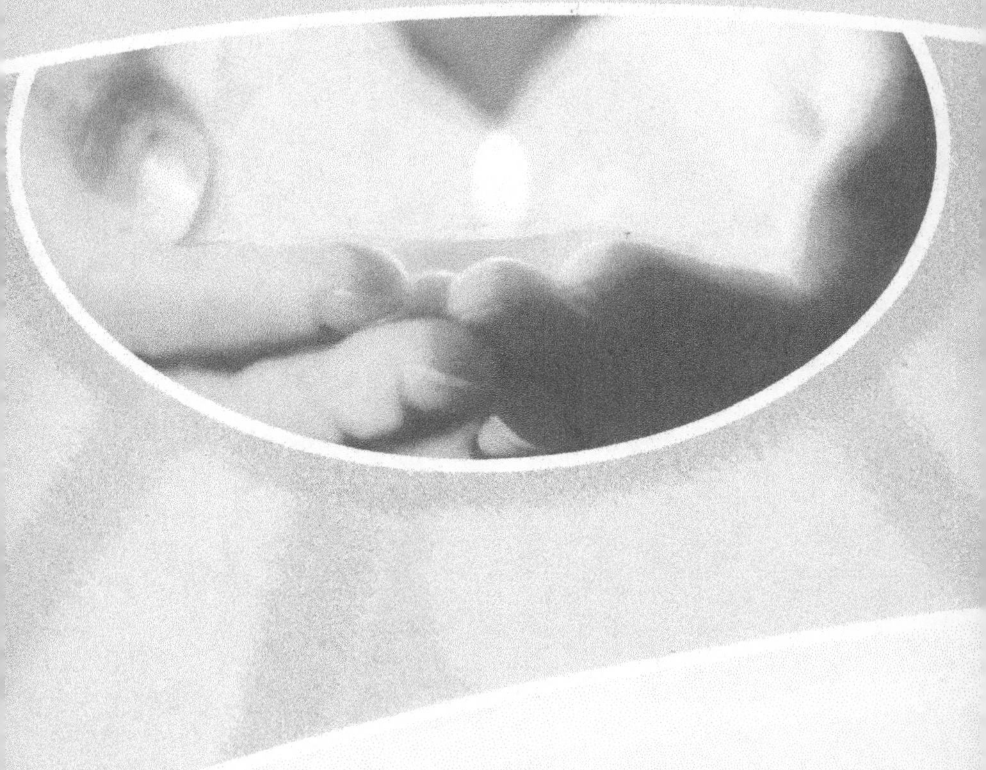

COUNTERING RELIGIOUS EXTREMISM: The Healing Power of Spiritual Friendships

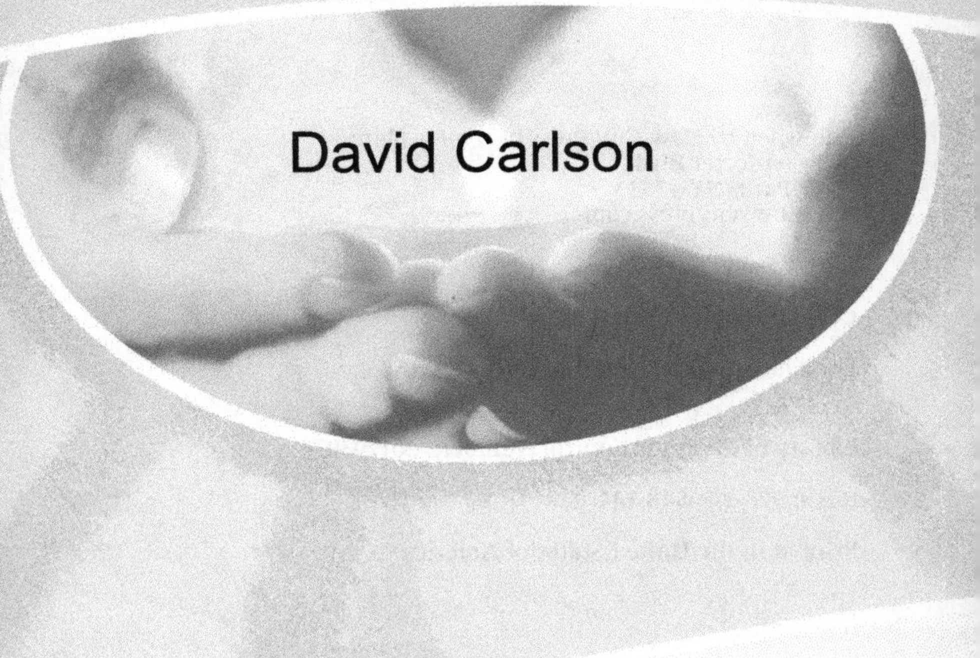

David Carlson

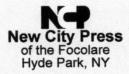

New City Press
of the Focolare
Hyde Park, NY

Published by New City Press of the Focolare
202 Comforter Blvd.,
Hyde Park, NY 12538
www.newcitypress.com

Cover design by Nick Cianfarani

Book design and layout by Steven Cordiviola

Library of Congress Control Number: 2017930349

ISBN: 978-1-56548-614-0

Printed in the United States of America

CONTENTS

DEDICATION

This book is dedicated to the memory of Lisa Morrison whose passion was building bridges of understanding between peoples of faith.

It is also dedicated to the Spiritual Oneness Group in Indianapolis, Indiana, the Interfaith Forum of Columbus, Indiana, and all such groups that shine a bright light of hope for the world's future.

PROLOGUE
AND
INTRODUCTION

PROLOGUE: THE CHALLENGE FACING US

When the second semester of the college year ended in May of 2014, I wondered whether it was time to stop teaching a course that I have offered for ten years. Perhaps, I thought, the course's topic—Religion and Violence—was a bit shopworn, a bit overworked.

And then ISIS (the Islamic State of Iraq and Syria)–also known as ISIL (the Islamic State of Iraq and the Levant)—exploded on the scene. Within a matter of days, I realized that religion and violence had again become *the* topic, more important now than ever.

I also realized something else. ISIS/ISIL's vision, which the West has finally grasped is frighteningly attractive to young people around the world, is the complete opposite of another future that is dawning.

ISIS/ISIL envisions reclaiming Syria, Iraq, and the Levant (the nations bordering the eastern shore of the Mediterranean Sea), a part of the world that was once both Islamic and part of an expansive and powerful empire. ISIS/ISIL is fighting to remove from "their world" the last vestiges of Western influence, an unwanted influence that ISIS/ISIL believes has humiliated Muslims at every turn of recent history. ISIS/ISIL believes that only then can the region fully live out God's will, which the group understands to be a severe and rigid interpretation of Islam.

ISIS/ISIL has odd parallels in the United States, Europe, and elsewhere. When extremists in such places think of the glory of this country, they picture a time in the past when the majority was almost entirely white, English-speaking, and Christian. They also wish to remove from "their world" newcomers who have come in search of freedom and economic possibilities. Similar sentiments against Arabs can be found among Jewish extremists in Israel, even as such sentiments are found among those who oppose Zionism. Some even believe that ridding their country of Muslims, Jews, Arabs, or other minorities and creating cultural and religious uniformity is doing the will of God.

Despite these narrow visions, ISIS/ISIL and other extremists have succeeded in recruiting followers. In ISIS/ISIL's case, their recruits have come from around the world, including the West. ISIS/ISIL's vision is proving to be compelling and therefore alarming. The same can be said for extremists in the United States, Europe, Israel, and elsewhere as they also have been successful in recruiting vulnerable youth. In *Terror in the Name of God: Why Militants Kill,* Jessica Stern argues that those who believe that their tribe or community has been humiliated or displaced are more likely to be attracted by the promise of "dehumiliation;" that is, actions, often violent, that seek to remove that humiliation and put history right.[1]

One of the main sources for ISIS/ISIL's early success in Syria and Iraq is found in this drive for "dehumiliation." The fact that beheading representatives from Western countries has *helped* ISIS/ISIL recruit rather than scare off young people is understandable in this context—ISIS/ISIL's extreme actions prove that it will not compromise with the West. For ISIS/ISIL, the humiliation stops now.

As the world considers how to respond to extremists such as ISIS/ISIL, Al-Qaeda, Al-Nusra, and Boko Haram, it is vital to remember that most Muslims consider such radical visions a dangerous distortion of Islam. Sheik Abdullah bin Bayyah, a respected cleric, takes this position in his recent *fatwah* (denouncement) of ISIS/ISIL. Still other observers, both Muslim and non-Muslim, view ISIS/ISIL's goal not only as a misinterpretation of Islam but also as a fruitless attempt to reverse history. While many Muslims might agree that during colonial and now post-colonial times in the Middle East Islam has been humiliated and betrayed by the West, they want no part of ISIS/ISIL's rigid and extreme new "state."

The same can be said of extremists in the United States, Europe, Israel, and elsewhere in the world. From the Ku Klux Klan to more recent white supremacist groups in the United States to radical Zionist groups in Israel and anti-Semitic groups in the Middle East and elsewhere, such perspectives are anathema to the majority of Christians, Muslims, and Jews despite the fact that their actions may be baptized in religious language and symbolism.

Yet in a superficial sense, such extremists are sensing something that is true—the future will be far different from the present. A "you leave me alone and I'll leave you alone" stance that privatizes religious faith and promotes benign tolerance leaves humanity ill-equipped to handle the intercultural and interreligious interactions that increasingly characterize the modern world.

Furthermore, in the case of ISIS/ISIL and extremists in the United States, Europe, and elsewhere, the present state of the world *is* part of the problem. ISIS/ISIL is able to attract recruits from around the world through its damning assessment of Western culture and values. Extremists in the West and the Middle East also see their radical dreams as the only alternative to the banality and sins of secularity and materialism. Such perspectives reject the tendency of modern nations to seek the will of the people, not what they maintain is the will of God.

An increasing number of young people around the world are susceptible to these extreme visions, as can be seen in the determination on the faces of these recruits. The ISIS/ISIL recruits and American, European, Israeli, and other Middle Eastern youth who are joining such causes may appear terrifying, but their vibrancy contrasts with the flatness in the faces of many others in the West— the faces of *haute couture* models in fashionable magazines, the faces of a great many American college students slumped in desks in packed lecture halls, or the faces of subway commuters.

Extremists recruit young people by promising that they will make history. This appeal works, as such promises exploit their sense of lethargy and malaise in the West. And lest we dismiss this critique of the West as uninformed, baseless, or simplistic, we should recall that Pope Benedict XVI also has diagnosed Western culture as tired, depressed, and divorced from its spiritual roots.[2]

There is, however, another vision of the future, one that neither concedes the future to God-absent materialism or religious extremism. *Countering Religious Extremism: The Healing Power of Spiritual Friendships* profiles how diverse peoples of faith are coming together, a way of life that rejects both conversionist competition (without succumbing to relativism) as well the unacceptably low hurdle of tolerance. This alternative future, this "third way," is embraced by Muslims, Christians, Jews, Sikhs, Buddhists, Hindus, and people who adhere to other faiths or to no faith at all. And the look on their faces is also vibrant, for they too sense that they are making history

The phrase "spiritual friendship" might sound innocuous if it conjures up images of people sitting around a cozy room with punch and cookies. That type of occasional being together is hardly a credible antidote to extremism. In fact, the concept of spiritual friendship is anything but bland and placid. This type of relationship makes great demands but offers great rewards. In truth, spiritual friendships offer a vision of the future as radical as those of the extremists.

Extremist groups often begin with a regional vision that can quickly become international in scope. The same is true of spiritual friendships. While at present these friendships are found primarily in Western societies, participants believe that this depth of relationship and encouragement will one day flourish in the Middle East, Africa, Southeast Asia, and other current "hot spots."

The West must recognize that vibrant extremist ideologies can be countered and defeated only by a better, sounder, and equally vibrant ideology. Military or police action may actually drive impressionable individuals into the arms of extremists.

Young people who turn away from soulless Western materialism need a stronger spiritual vision than extremism. Extremist utopian visions always end up in stifling uniformity and isolation. In contrast, spiritual friendships acknowledge, yes, even celebrate, religious diversity. They offer a future of new and life-enriching possibilities, where across religious lines people of faith encourage one another to live more compassionately; where, without sacrificing their distinctiveness, peoples of faith cooperate in purposeful and healing action and give birth to new methods of defusing religious suspicion and hatred.

No one can predict what the next decades will bring. Will ISIS/ISIL collapse from within as have so many other extremist movements? Will extremists in our own country continue to proliferate? Will extremist leaders overreach themselves and unleash a Taliban-like society where no one is allowed to express an independent thought? What will happen when recruits return home or when they want to "de-recruit?"

Imagining a future with flourishing spiritual friendships is far more pleasing, and these friendships will not be restricted to the West alone. The globalization, mobility, and technological advances that affect the entire world (although at different rates and often in the service of materialism) provide an opportunity, greater than ever before, for people of diverse faiths to meet. And as the world's demographics change, this contact will not be merely virtual, but actual. As will become clear from the chapters that follow, diverse communities already exist where the "religious other" is perceived not as a threat but as a gift of God.

Western secularism and materialism will not die out soon, but they have failed to counter extremism at home and abroad. Indeed, these Western traits fuel extremism. Spiritual friendships can provide a remedy. Partners in spiritual friendships know that religious tension, hatred, and violence need not be humanity's future. They know that the healing power of religion is just dawning, and this power can transform the lives of individuals. Between peoples of faith, religions can build not walls of separation but bridges of understanding. Such bridge building is essential in providing a viable alternative to religious extremism.

Our world is at the dawning of interreligious encouragement. This understanding and encouragement is not to be confused with religious convergence or conformity. Those interviewed for *Countering Religious Extremism: The Healing Power of Spiritual Friendships* believe that the future will not bring an amalgamation of the world into a bland whole. The world's religions will remain distinct—intact and respected. Yet more and more, religious isolation will give way to spiritual friendships between diverse peoples of faith.

Countering Religious Extremism: The Healing Power of Spiritual Friendships invites readers on a journey. Those interviewed for this book have already built bridges of understanding and have crossed them into a far better future, one superior to the vision of extremism or Western materialism. We call on people who love their faith to join us.

THOSE MOHAMMEDANS

I Might As Well Have Been Blind

IT IS HIGHLY UNLIKELY that someone like me would ever have entered into spiritual friendships with Muslims, Jews, Buddhists, Sikhs and Hindus. The person I was as recently as fifteen years ago would be surprised, no, shocked, at the path that I now follow.

In the mid-sixties I attended high school in north-central Illinois, where religious diversity meant that some of my classmates were Methodist, Baptist, Lutheran, or Catholic. There were three Jewish students in my school, but I knew no Muslims, or "Mohammedans," as textbooks at that time often labeled followers of Islam: "Morocco has an annual rainfall of x inches, is rich in mineral deposits, and the people are Mohammedans."

From history books, I pictured "Mohammedans" as robed warriors astride horses or camels. With their curved swords these enemies of my faith had fought and eventually defeated the Christian Crusaders.

In hindsight, I find it revealing that I was never asked to consider "Islam" or "Muslims" in my United States history classes. I grew up with no sense of Muslims being part of our country's religious landscape. Even with the rise in the sixties of Malcolm X and the Black Muslims, those angry men and women seemed to be threats, not members of our society.

The one exception was Muhammad Ali, whose life story from his boxing days until his death inspired me as a youth and continues to inspire me. Ali was undoubtedly the first Muslim whom I (and I doubt that I was alone) observed praying, which he did routinely in his corner of the boxing ring even as the crowd was screaming and sometimes booing behind him.

While it might seem that I grew up in some rural backwater area of the American Midwest, my hometown is actually a midsize city with a fairly large public university. I knew a few international students, but they were Christians who attended the Baptist church my father pastored. I also had an after-school job in a grocery store, one frequented by numerous college students. Hindu, Muslim, and Buddhist students and faculty from the university either did not frequent my neighborhood grocery or were invisible to me.

A Sheltered College Experience

College is intended to be an opening-out experience—intellectually, socially, and personally. I attended Wheaton College, Billy Graham's alma mater, which many consider to be the foremost evangelical college in the country. Wheaton promised a spiritually enriching college experience. Every student, faculty member, and staff person signed a pledge which delineated not only the expected moral behavior but also the college's conservative brand of Christian faith. During my college years I knew no Muslim fellow students, had no Muslim instructors, nor did I hear a Muslim speaker.

Wheaton College was, and remains, committed to fulfilling the Great Commission, to spread the gospel of Jesus Christ around the world before His glorious return. I was also raised with this belief, that the world could be divided into those who knew Jesus Christ, the son of God, and those who needed to know him.

My college years offered no opportunity to encounter Muslims. What I did learn about Islam characterized it as the religion of backward countries in the Middle East, countries that threatened Israel and barred Christian missionaries. In college, however, I did hear stories of courageous missionaries who, with the daring of international spies, smuggled Bibles into Islamic countries and even held secret prayer meetings and Bible studies.

Had I been asked at the time, I would have lumped Muslims in with those who were afraid to let people think and decide for themselves, like the Communists. And in that, I would not have been totally wrong. Some Islamic countries continue to prohibit other religions from being practiced and shared openly. But I did not know then that in Islam these prohibitions are not universal and are at odds with the Qur'an's admonishment that religion cannot be coerced (Sura 2:256). Nor did I know at the time that Christianity, particularly in Spain and other European countries where the Christian faith was dominant, had once established similar prohibitions that barred Jews and Muslims from freely sharing their "gospel," their good news, and practicing their faith.

Much later, I realized how much my view of Islam during these years was both typical and culturally-determined. The West has long viewed Islam as backward and undeveloped, and judged Muslims as untruthful, unable to govern themselves, and generally lacking reason.[3] Yes, Judaism could be included in the category of a "Western" religion, but Islam? The Islam portrayed in *National Geographic* photos seemed closer to Hinduism than to the Midwestern Protestantism with which I had grown up. I couldn't understand how anyone could possibly be attracted to this religion.

Traveling with Blinders On

My first direct encounter with Muslims came in 1975 when, immediately following doctoral studies in Scotland, I was hired by an evangelical college to serve as lecturer to students traveling to Israel. Despite the fact that I had never before traveled to the Middle East, I was not about to turn down such an opportunity.

I had done my doctoral work in New Testament studies, so in approaching the Holy Land I made sure that we "did Israel" almost entirely as the land of Old Testament heroes and Jesus. In that way, I fulfilled the expectations of the evangelical college's program while not venturing beyond my intellectual limitations.

Finding Jesus in modern Israel is not easy, however, as the land is sacred to Jews, Muslims, and numerous Christian denominations. American evangelicals find many of those denominations as foreign as other religions. Jerusalem itself contains an Arab Quarter, numerous Jewish areas, Christian quarters, and even an Armenian area. Our college group stayed in an Episcopal hospice near King David's Gate, where we were told that some of the custodians and cafeteria personnel were Muslim converts to Christianity. One night during our stay, passing a room where a small number of these workers were being led in a Bible study, I was struck by a sadness or loneliness that seemed to emanate from the room. In that moment, I saw these men and women as exiles, no longer welcome in the quarters of the city that had once been their homes.

The sense of "historical vertigo" I experienced in Jerusalem differs from what I have felt in cities such as Rome or Athens. There, the ancient sites compete with the noise and pace of modern life. But in Jerusalem, the city of Jesus' passion, death, and resurrection competes not so much with modernity but with the holy sites of the other two western religions. In Jerusalem the most sacred Jewish site, the Western Wall (also called the "Wailing Wall"), is only blocks away from the Church of the Holy Sepulcher (the traditional site of Jesus' crucifixion and resurrection) and directly below the two mosques (Dome of the Rock and Al-Aqsa) built atop the traditional Jewish Temple Mount. In a six-block area, crowds of Jewish, Christian and Muslim pilgrims elbow one another, trying to find enough space and quiet to breathe in their faith's founding stories.

Looking back on my time in Israel, I admit that our evangelical group saw only what we could understand.

Following guides who were local Christians, we scurried through crowds of "others" to sites where I would lecture on pertinent Christian texts and stories. Our group was largely oblivious as we walked by locations sacred to Muslims or Jews. The Jews, Muslims, and even the Palestinian Christians whom we passed on the streets, in the markets, or at the airport seemed more remote to us than did Jesus and the disciples.

Can You Coach Soccer?

Three years after my time in Israel, and after a stint counseling troubled teenagers in a Catholic hospital, I was hired by a church-affiliated college in south-central Indiana. For the most part, my students at Franklin College had the same limited background in religious diversity that I had growing up in Illinois.

The one exception to this uniformity in my first years at Franklin was a group of Bengali students who had somehow washed up at this Indiana school and wished to play soccer. Because I had lived in Scotland and loved Scottish football—soccer, that is—they assumed that I knew the game well enough to serve as coach. And so I met the first Muslims I knew as friends—Faisal, Faruk, Mamoon and Mamoud—students who had forgotten more about soccer than I would ever know.

What struck me most about these young men was their ease in their new American surroundings, even though I knew that on and off campus they occasionally experienced prejudice.

As my young family lived on campus, the Bengalis often visited us, especially on the weekends when many of the Indiana students went home. What I remember most is the laughter, often directed at Midwestern American behaviors that would never have occurred in Bangladesh or even Scotland. We also laughed at behaviors in Bangladesh and Scotland that would be funny to Midwesterners. If we were laughing *at* anything or anyone, it would not have been our countries of origin or where we had lived, but at our common experience of the world as both familiar and foreign.

Did we every discuss religion or theology? No, but in laughing and eating together, we did create a type of spiritual connection. I certainly felt their respect for me as a Christian which, at the time, I did not understand but willingly accepted. I hope they felt the same from my family.

A Green Professor with Little to Profess

During my early years at Franklin College, I was assigned to teach "Living Religions West," a course that introduced students to the historical roots and contemporary expressions of Judaism, Christianity, and Islam. It is telling that I felt comfortable (falsely so, it turned out) teaching Christianity and Judaism and hesitant only about teaching Islam.

In a sense, I approached this course with the same gaps of knowledge that I had experienced three years before in Israel. From my doctoral studies I knew something of Biblical Judaism and intertestamental Judaism, but little of rabbinic Judaism, of Judaism under Christian and Muslim domination, of Judaism as the scapegoat of Christian Europe, of Kabbalistic and Hasidic Judaism, of Judaism in the Enlightenment, and only bits of Judaism in the blood-soaked twentieth century. In truth, I was comfortable only with Biblical Judaism and the most common Holocaust accounts.

But I knew less about Islam. On the few occasions when I had tried to read the Qur'an, I could make little sense of it. The suras, or chapters, seemed a mix of the dullness of Leviticus cast in the repetitious rhythms of the Psalms. And yet, here I was, responsible for introducing Islam objectively to Midwestern college students.

Despite these drawbacks, that semester I managed to do one thing right in regard to Islam. I built into the course a field trip to the North American Islamic Center in Plainfield, Indiana, an experience that turned out to be both helpful and disorienting.

Religious zeal and conviction can be powerful forces, which most Americans and Europeans meet in the "on-fire" variety of Christians. When Americans think of evangelism or of hearing someone offer a "testimony," they usually picture conservative Christians—fundamentalists and evangelicals. At the mosque in Plainfield, I saw some of my students' faces pale as an African-American convert to Islam shared with us his journey to finding God and then his confident claim that Islam is the fulfillment of both Judaism and Christianity. His knowledge of the New Testament was impressive, even as he wove verses of our Bible together in ways that we had never encountered before as Christians.

On the memorable van ride back to campus from the mosque, students who sat in stunned silence during the convert's talk were now bursting with questions and comments. As I concentrated on the road, I could feel their need for me to discount what we had heard, to point out the flaws and falsehoods in the convert's testimony. But during the visit to the Islamic Center my own sense of faith and conviction had shifted. In the Muslim convert with the piercing eyes and certainty of voice and faith, we met a true evangelist, a type of Muslim Billy Graham. Zeal, conviction, and evangelistic fire were no longer the sole prerogatives of Christianity—and that had been a shocking experience.

That field trip served as a touchstone as I, for the first time, began to consider Islam as the compelling path by which over a billion people find a meaningful life. I was not particularly interested in the issues of headscarves or ayatollahs, although Iran's Ayatollah Khomeini scared me. Instead, I was impressed as I learned of certain Islamic practices, such as praying five times a day. Why did I assume as a Christian that God expected me to pray once a day—or even less? I also sensed that the Islamic understanding of sin as being human tendencies to worship something else in place of God or to be forgetful of God—something I was very good at—was spiritually astute.

But while I held a deeper respect for the Islam that I was encountering in our textbooks, I still did not know a Muslim on a personal spiritual level.

Running Toward the Fire

A recent advertisement for the United States Marine Corps shows a band of soldiers running toward a massive explosion. The voice-over conveys the message that a Marine runs *toward* a catastrophe, not *away* from it. In the wake of the events of September 11, 2001 (which is most commonly referred to as "9/11"), many Americans chose to run *away* from Islam, from understanding even the basic beliefs of 1.6 billion people in the world. But 9/11 affected me in the opposite way. I knew, both as a professor of religious studies and as a Christian, that after 9/11 I needed to run *toward* the new religious challenges facing the world, and that meant running *toward* Muslims.

After several semesters of offering a course on "Religion and Violence," I sensed that my students were gaining necessary knowledge of the background to the terror attacks in 2001 and the cultural and religious tensions surfacing in our post-9/11 world. But my students seemed to want something else from me—a solution—and I had none. They were asking me the same question that was plaguing me: *Is there any hope?*

In 2006, I decided to search for an answer. Some of my friends thought it strange when I began to travel the country interviewing monks and nuns. Yet, from my previous interviews at monasteries, I knew these men and women would have processed 9/11 and its aftermath in different ways than did mainstream American culture. I began these interviews with the hope that these thoughtful Christians would share their perspectives on how we as American Christians had responded—and should have responded.

Those interviews formed the basis of *Peace Be with You: Monastic Wisdom for a Terror-Filled World* (Thomas Nelson, 2011). By the end I was radically changed. A three-year journey that began with a simple question—how did monks and nuns respond to 9/11?—became a personal search for a new understanding of forgiveness, one that would stand the test of our troubled post-9/11 world. Yet, while any discussions of the rise of religious hatred and violence could not ignore Islam, Islam rarely came up as a focus of the interviews.

Throughout that journey, I was accompanied in spirit by the Trappist monk Thomas Merton. In an unexpected but life-changing moment in downtown Louisville in 1958, Merton found himself in a shopping district, a location that to a non-materialistic Trappist monk easily could have seemed like hell. Instead of revulsion or condemnation, Merton had this unexpected reaction:

> In Louisville, at the corner of Fourth and Walnut, in the center of the shopping district, I was suddenly overwhelmed with the realization that I loved all those people, that they were mine and I theirs, that we could not be alien to one another even though we were total strangers. It was like waking from a dream of separateness, of spurious self-isolation in a special world, the world of renunciation and supposed holiness. The whole illusion of a separate holy existence is a dream. Not that I question the reality of my vocation, or of my monastic life: but the conception of "separation from the world" that we have in the monastery too easily presents itself as a total illusion: the illusion that by making vows we become a separate species of beings, pseudoangels, "spiritual men," men of interior life, what have you...
>
> I have the immense joy of being man, a member of a race in which God Himself became incarnate...
>
> Then it was as if I suddenly saw the secret beauty of their hearts, where neither sin nor desire nor self-

> knowledge can reach, the core of their reality, the person that each one is in God's eyes.[4]

Those few moments in Louisville changed Merton's life. While never abandoning his monastic vows, including the Trappist vow of separation from ordinary society, Merton took a new "vow of conversation," as he titled one of his subsequent books, with the world. He began conversations with Christian, Jewish, Muslim, and Buddhist leaders, as well as non-religious writers and poets. Even the Iron Curtain could not limit his new engagement with the world.

For Merton the epiphany in Louisville brought a new understanding of Christ's presence in the world:

> "If we believe in the Incarnation of the Son of God, there should be no one on earth in whom we are not prepared to see, in mystery, the presence of Christ."[5]

Somehow, this belief that Christ could be found in everyone spoke directly to my confusion and despair after 9/11. In *Peace Be with You: Monastic Wisdom for a Terror-Filled World,* I wrote,

> I believe this entire project could be summarized in this prayer: that every person in the world would have Merton's Fourth-and-Walnut Street epiphany. What would happen in our world if, just for one human second, we would be given the grace to see our neighbors—the leaders of this world, the radio talk show crazies, and our own enemies in that light of truth?[6]

Throughout the interviews that I conducted in 2007, I quickly grasped that Merton's epiphany was not new, but was an expression of the ancient monastic Rule of St. Benedict, chapter 53: "Let all guests who arrive be received as Christ, because He will say, 'I was a stranger and you took me in' (Mt 25:35)."

What would happen, I wondered, if Merton's epiphany was meant not just for monks, but for all of us? And what would happen if I saw Christ in everyone I met? Almost as an experiment, I began to close my days with a new prayer: "Where did I meet You today?" What I came to realize is as startling as it is simple—in each person I had met Christ.

As I was beginning to live with this new perspective, something unplanned occurred. I had expected that *Peace Be with You: Monastic Wisdom for a Terror-Filled World* would bring new conversations with Christians who were challenged or even troubled by the book. I was unprepared for the reaction of a friend, a noted American Muslim scholar, who was interested in my interviews. Dr. Khadija Khaja's evaluation of *Peace Be with You* flabbergasted me. In her opinion, my interviews with Christian monks and nuns offered an opening with people of other faiths that Muslims "had been waiting to read."

Dr. Khaja's reaction served to end my monastic interview project with another prompting. In talking further about the interfaith implications of my book, Dr. Khaja and I came to a startling but mutual conclusion: *What American Muslims need most from American Christians is for them to be better Christians, and what American Christians need most from American Muslims is for them to be better Muslims.*

After the publication of the book, the more I repeated this challenging conclusion in my public talks the more I felt led to act on this prompting. What kinds of approaches, I wondered, could bring the Muslims and Christians together, where people of faith could support and encourage one another?

Of course, others had asked these questions long before I had, and I had already participated in two interfaith venues that were popular after 9/11 and remain popular today. Unfortunately, both of these gatherings have left me disappointed. One of them occurred in academic settings, where scholars from diverse religious backgrounds presented papers. I left these conferences feeling let down, knowing that our densely-worded, erudite presentations would have little to no impact on the general culture.

I had also attended a second type of interfaith gathering; meet-and-greet opportunities that brought together ministers, rabbis, priests, and imams for an evening of informal discussion about a shared social concern. While I found these occasional meetings pleasant, I sensed that whatever relationships were formed on these occasions were unlikely to lead to enduring cultural change.

I wanted to be part of something powerful, something that would influence the relationship of ordinary Christians and Muslims. What I was seeking to enter were spiritual friendships between religious communities, ways of being together on a regular basis for the purpose of encouraging one another on our faith journeys.

I shared my desire for such a friendship with Dr. Khaja, who wisely suggested that we visit the mosques in Indianapolis to meet the Muslim leaders of our city. Although we had no definite goal, Dr. Khaja and I both felt that something important could result from these conversations.

Something important did result. I began to meet Muslims, Christians, and then others who were already involved in precisely what I was searching for—strong friendships where issues of religious faith were not avoided, where people of diverse beliefs had the opportunity to share the importance of faith in their lives.

When I subsequently entered spiritual friendships for myself, I was astonished by the effect on me. The more I participated, the more Muslims, Jews, Sikhs, Buddhists and others encouraged me to deepen my faith as a Christian and to live a more Christ-like life.

On the basis of those experiences, a new question began to form in my mind: "What have I missed by *not* establishing spiritual friendships with people of other faiths?"

This book is the record of the spiritual gifts, the treasures that I and others have received from spiritual friendships. These experiences give me hope that religious extremism, such as that promulgated by ISIS/ISIL as well as by hate groups in our own country, will not be the world's future.

A FRIENDSHIP LONG DELAYED

All professors hope that something they say in class will be remembered. It is difficult, however, to imagine that such a memory would survive for forty years.

So, as I began to envision establishing spiritual friendships with Muslims, it seemed odd to me that one name repeatedly came to mind. As far as I could remember, I had heard of Frank Laubach only once, during a class in seminary forty-three years earlier. I do not remember the class; neither do I remember the professor. But Laubach's name would not leave me and, in hindsight, I believe this was providential. For in Frank Laubach, I found a worthy guide for my new spiritual venture.

In the 1920s and 30s, Frank Laubach was a Presbyterian missionary to the Moros, a Muslim tribe in the Philippines. Tragically, this same region is again in the news because religious violence between religious communities persists. Unsurprisingly, Laubach's first reaction to Islam in the Philippines of the 1920s was not favorable. As a Christian missionary in a predominantly Muslim area, he would hardly have been welcomed. In one of his early writings, an article published only eight years after he was commissioned as a missionary to the Philippines, his frustration is apparent: "Islam was introduced about the year 1450 by Abu Bakr who claimed to be a direct descendent from Muhammad and who declared himself Sultan of the Moros. Abu Bakr poured into an already war-loving race the fanatic and aggressive doctrine of Islam."[7]

Laubach's early assessment of Islam as "aggressive" and "fanatical" resembles the language that some American TV evangelists currently use to describe Muslims. But subsequently, his attitude changed as he took the unusual step of joining Muslims in prayer as well as listening to and learning from them. In the process, he experienced a breakthrough in his spiritual life that can be summarized as living increasingly in God-consciousness.

"Living in the atmosphere of Islam is proving—thus far—a tremendous spiritual stimulus."[8] Laubach wrote these words on January 20, 1930, after fifteen years of working and living closely with the Moro people and seven years after writing his earlier, negative assessment of Islam. Something in his contacts with the Moros had transformed his attitude toward Islam. What he had judged to be a "fanatic and aggressive doctrine" became a "tremendous spiritual stimulus," and I was keen to find out what lay behind this conversion. While he did not mention particular Muslims by name, Laubach's new approach seemed nothing less than an application of Islamic God-consciousness to the Christian ideal of living in the Kingdom of God. "Frank Laubach spoke particularly of what he learned from Islam's emphasis on the submission of the will to God—which is the moment of entry into the Kingdom when the individual will submits itself to God's will."[9]

In rediscovering Laubach, I felt that I had met a friend, someone who shared my journey. He was a providential sign urging me forward on my quest to establish spiritual friendships with Muslims. He offered me a clear model and definition of spiritual friendship: *a true spiritual friendship is a friendship marked by two movements of the spirit—the sharing of God's love with the faith partner and the receiving of God's love from that same partner. In this relationship, each partner encourages the other on his or her spiritual journey.*

Jesus said a good tree is known by its good fruit (Mt 12:22), so I was moved when Laubach wrote that his spiritual friendships with Muslims had benefited not just him but Muslims as well. "Take Lanao and the Moros, for illustration. Their responsiveness is to me a continuous source of amazement. I do nothing that I can see excepting to pray for them, and to walk among them, thinking of God. They know I am a Protestant. Yet two of the leading Moslem priests have gone around the province telling everybody that I would help the people to know God"[10] No matter how many times I read these words, I am stunned by the image of a Christian missionary and Muslim imams sharing spiritual friendship.

What Laubach discovered in the Philippines of the 1930s remains the greatest spiritual need of our contemporary world. Building bridges of understanding and encouragement between Muslims, Christians, Jews, and others, and not just settling for religious tolerance, is essential to establish lasting peace. The spiritual friendship between Laubach and the Moro people proves that religious fault lines can be spanned. In the 1920s and 30s, Muslims and Christians, faithful to their traditions, recognized that they could "help [one another] to know God." What happened in the Philippines nearly a century ago can happen again.

Laubach's brief journal is well worth reading. There is candor, hope, and spiritual wisdom in every entry. Certainly, one of the journal's most significant contributions is its exposing the irrational fear that many still have about interfaith relations. This all-too-common fear is that the path of interfaith dialogue or spiritual friendships leads to religious relativism. The journal dispels that fear. Laubach was a committed Christian, yet a Christian who, without compromise, was open to Islam. His writings demonstrate that openness to Islam did not make him less, but rather more of a Christian.

MY FIRST LESSON IN ISLAM

Once I committed to seeking spiritual friendships with Muslims, my attitude toward Islam took a subtle but important shift. In my courses I have always worked diligently to emphasize that no one has the right to judge a religion without coming to understand how to its followers that religion is a path to a meaningful life. With that stance, I have sought to dispel the untruths that many people carry around about other religions. Nevertheless, when I began to envision entering into spiritual friendships with Muslims, I realized that I would need something other than evenhandedness. Now I wanted to understand how Islam could help me find more meaning in my life as a Christian.

My first experience with this new mindset came early in 2013, within the first two weeks of my Introduction to Religion course. In order to impress my students with how the religious world had changed after 9/11, I began the course, as I had for several years, by focusing on the philosophy of Al-Qaeda. Instead of coming to know what the attackers believed about God, about what humans should be living for, and about what the future might hold, in the United States we had focused on Al-Qaeda's tactics. One of my main goals was that my students realize the difference between Al-Qaeda and ISIS/ISIL, and the normative Islam practiced by the majority of Muslims in the world. My students were helped greatly by the National Geographic film *Inside Mecca*, produced in the wake of 9/11 with the clear intention of helping non-Muslims understand the appeal of

Islam to people around the world, including those in the United States.

Inside Mecca follows the experiences of three Muslims—an Irish Catholic convert from Texas, a South African DJ, and a Malaysian businessman—as they prepare for the Hajj, the prescribed pilgrimage to Mecca. Given that non-Muslims are forbidden to visit Mecca, the film (shot entirely by Muslims) offers a rare glimpse of the pilgrimage's pageantry and transforming experience. Although I had shown the film several times before, when I watched it in the spring of 2013, I was drawn to a comment made by Kahlil, the black South African DJ. In Mecca for the first time, Khalil was disappointed at the racism he encountered. He battled his frustration by keeping in mind the requirement of the Hajj that he remain in a state of sanctity called *ihram.*

Ihram refers to the simple white garments worn by men on the Hajj. In the dress of *ihram*, their worldly status does not matter as they stand as equals before God. But *ihram* is more than clothing. It also connotes the spiritual state of devotion to be retained during the Hajj. In *ihram*, a Muslim seeks to avoid anger, gossip, frustration, and all the negative states that seem to arise so naturally when we feel attacked or vulnerable. Of course, it could be argued that *ihram* should be the condition of a faithful Muslim at all times, but devoting a season to seeking a pure heart with intense fervor seems spiritually sound. Of course, it is far easier to change one's clothes than to change one's mind and heart. That is the true battle. That is the deeper *ihram.*

Ihram *and the Season of Lent*

As an Orthodox Christian, my season of Lent (the forty days prior to Easter Sunday) was beginning at the point when I showed *Inside Mecca*. The juxtaposition of the film and Lent helped me realize that *ihram* has several similarities to the attitudes expected of Christians during this season of reflection and repentance. Lent is a journey of the soul, in a way, a Christian Hajj. Its purpose is to help the observer become more Christ-like and to exhibit more fully the fruits of the Holy Spirit. And those gifts include patience and self-control (Gal 5:22-26), virtues similar to that of *ihram*.

As Lent began, I committed to observing *ihram,* to dealing with my negative emotions, particularly the urge to gossip and be judgmental. From my previous career in counseling, I knew that to be healthy, *ihram* could not simply be suppression. Rather, *ihram* must mean meeting negative feelings with patience and even with longsuffering. As the weeks of Lent passed, I became increasingly aware of the resonance between *ihram* and the Prayer of St. Ephrem that Orthodox Christians recite only during Lent:

> O Lord and Master of my life, take from me the spirit of sloth, despair, lust for power, and idle talk. But give rather the spirit of chastity, humility, patience, and love to Thy servant. Yes, O Lord and King, grant me to see my own transgressions, and not to judge my brother, for blessed are Thou, unto ages and ages. Amen

Through St. Ephrem's beautiful prayer, I understand that Lent, much as *ihram* during the Hajj, requires me to focus on the sinner whom I know best—myself. I am encouraged to focus on the log in my own eye rather than the speck in another's.

A second benefit of keeping *ihram* in mind during Lent was that in avoiding gossip and being judgmental, I began to see other people not just in a different light, but in a clearer light. I suspect that our human tendency to pick out others' foibles is born out of a fear that our own weaknesses will make us unacceptable. And so, fearing rejection, we take comfort in looking down on others. In so doing, we miss the truth about others, a truth that became more apparent to me during Lent that year. Everyone we know or even pass on the street is a unique being at some stage of an unrepeatable story. Everyone is a miraculous and sacred being, "walking around shining like the sun," as Thomas Merton saw in Louisville in 1958.

Pondering *ihram* during Lent of 2013 produced yet another unexpected outcome. One of the most moving Lenten texts is the story of Jesus dining at the home of Simon, the Pharisee (Lk 7:36-50). In the story, a woman of notorious background enters Simon's house uninvited and washes Jesus' feet with her tears and rubs them with ointment. Simon is offended and concludes that Jesus is certainly no true prophet. Knowing Simon's attitude, Jesus asks his host an amazing question. "Do you see this woman?" (Lk 7:44). On the surface, it seems unnecessary for Jesus to ask that question. Of course, Simon sees the woman. But at a deeper level, because of his prejudice, Simon has not truly seen the woman at all. He has seen only a sinner, not a person, and certainly not the person Jesus sees, a person overflowing with love. In Jesus' eyes, the woman is truly "shining like the sun." The discipline of practicing *ihram* during Lent by avoiding gossip helped me catch a glimpse of how God sees us. The woman, a known sinner, perhaps a prostitute, is revealed to be a saint. Simon, a respected religious leader of his community, is revealed to be spiritually impoverished. I ended Lent wondering how often I am like Simon, accepting the *apparently* real instead of seeing what is *truly* real about others.

On Pascha (Easter Sunday), my neighbor passed me the light of the resurrection from her candle before I passed the light on to others. The moment marked the end of my Lenten journey, one that deepened as I sought to live out more fully the Christian virtue of forbearance and the parallel Islamic virtue of *ihram*. Through them, I felt nearer to Christ than ever before. How could I deny that I was having an experience similar to Frank Laubach's? I could not deny that contact with Islam was deepening my Christian faith.

PART I:
MARWAN WAFA

AMERICA IS MY HOME

MOHAMMED IS HELPING ME. I have no more intention of giving up Christianity and becoming a Mohammedan than I had twenty years ago, but I find myself richer for the Islamic experience of God.[11]

> The final stage in the long history of Muslim-Christian relations is still in its beginnings. When it is fully realized, it will, we hope, lead to a recognition of Islam not as a heresy, but as an authentic expression of the divine and immutable truth. In this spirit of mutual recognition and appreciation, Islam may find something to teach Christians that would strengthen their own faith in the Truth.[12]

It might seem that I met Marwan Wafa by accident. A church in a nearby city had invited me to offer a four-week series on other faiths. I agreed to lead this series with one stipulation. Instead of lecturing about the religions that were becoming more visible in their city, I offered to facilitate an interfaith dialogue with local representatives of Judaism, Islam, Hinduism, and Buddhism. I did not live in this city and did not know the best representatives of the different faith communities, but I did know many of the interfaith leaders of that city, and through them I learned of Marwan and his daughter Ala'a. Marwan and Ala'a are easy to like. They are thoughtful, well-spoken, and caring. Their eyes are alive, their minds alert. I believe that all who attended the interfaith dialogue at the church were moved by the warm relationship and mutual respect between this father and daughter. Ala'a, wearing a headscarf, dispelled a common American assumption when she shared that her father had told her not to allow anyone to pressure her into wearing the headscarf.

By the end of the evening of dialogue with Marwan and Ala'a, I could tell that the Christian audience had gained an entirely new impression of Islam. I remember one woman who approached Ala'a after the dialogue and admitted apologetically that she had never actually talked with a Muslim before. Smiling, Ala'a put the woman at ease by responding, "I hear that all the time." What occurred that evening between the two women and between Marwan and me was not the forming of a spiritual friendship, but it was the beginning spark of one. For the spark that begins all spiritual friendships is this: the sudden awareness of the heart, even more than the head, that a person is looking into the eyes of someone, though different religiously, who is somehow yet deeply related to them spiritually.

Marwan and I have much in common. We are both roughly the same age and both have grown children. We both have careers in higher education, Marwan at that time an academic dean in the Indiana-Purdue Universities system and I a professor at Franklin College. I also appreciate his straight-talking approach as well as something that I had not anticipated: Marwan is a strong Muslim, but he is also someone with questions about his faith, as I have about mine.

In my email invitation to Marwan, I asked if we could meet monthly to explore spiritual friendships between Muslims and Christians. In his response the following day, he expressed his personal interest in connecting with friends "who share the same passion for spirituality and the love of fellow humans and their wellbeing." As I read that email, I felt all the emotions, from excitement to anxiety, of a new journey beginning. What would I learn from Marwan? Would Marwan learn anything from me? Would the conversations seem forced or artificial, or is a spiritual friendship across religious lines possible?

Our First Meeting

In February, 2013, we met in Marwan's comfortable, spacious office. The one-hour meeting I requested turned into a two-hour session. Throughout our time together, I sensed that Marwan was finding the experience as exciting and long-awaited as I did.

I began by asking how he came to be an academic dean in south-central Indiana. He explained that although born and raised in Kuwait, he is Palestinian. He described his family's second-class citizenship as Palestinian refugees in Kuwait, as well as their having been forced out of their village on the West Bank during the 1948 war with Israel. Knowing that his Palestinian ancestry curtailed his future in Kuwait, Marwan came to the United States to further his education. He intended to return to Kuwait but, as he said, "You fall in love with this place. The people are good. There are laws." After a pause, Marwan said sadly, "I love Americans and I hate the foreign policy of America." If I thought he might then vent about his family's trials at being Palestinian in America, I could not have been more wrong.

In Marwan, I met a man who has known a depth of homelessness that I could not even imagine. In traveling to Israel to visit his ancestral village, he had been treated suspiciously by security forces. Even when he returned to Kuwait, the country of his birth, Marwan had routinely been met repeated by the question, "Why are you here?"

"I always remember this," Marwan said, his voice softer. "When I got my permanent residency [in the United States], we visited Kuwait... So, when I come back, that was in New York, this guy [at passport control] was Asian-looking, so I think that maybe he'd been a naturalized or Hawaiian or his family roots from the

Far East, and he asked me 'where are you coming from' [and] 'what do you do.'" But then the immigration officer smiled and said words that Marwan had never heard before. "Welcome home." Marwan paused, fighting back tears. Those tears were not about the negative effects of U.S foreign policy on his people, but about how much America means to him. "I always get emotional when I think about that," he explained. "That was the most powerful thing that I have ever heard in my life."

As I left, I felt that we had learned something important about each other. Spiritual friendships begin much as any other friendship begins, with participants sharing the defining moments in their lives. I had shared my own journey from reading about Mohammedans as a high school student to my desire, after writing my first book, to establish spiritual friendships with Muslims. And Marwan had told me his story.

But through Marwan, I had also learned something about myself. As a child of the sixties, specifically the civil rights and youth movements, I am an American who always desires for my country to be better than it is. I still believe that those who love their country uncritically and blindly are committing a form of idolatry. Neither the United States, nor any nation, should ever be worshipped for what it is, but must be constantly challenged to live out its promises more fully. Consequently, whether I have been living outside the United States or at home in central Indiana, I tend to react to United States domestic and foreign policy decisions and think, "We can do better."

Marwan—a Muslim, a Palestinian, an immigrant, an American—taught me a valuable lesson. Here was a man who had more motive than I ever could have to resent America, particularly because of our foreign policy in the Middle East. Yet I had to admit that Marwan loves America in a different way than I do. His love is certainly not naïve, but is based on a far different "back story" than mine. I can recall only once while traveling abroad when an official questioned my reasons for being at a particular border, in Eastern Europe during the Cold War years. But such suspicion had been Marwan's recurring experience in Israel and Kuwait—until he became a citizen of this country. Only in the United States has he been "welcomed home."

I need to remember Marwan's experience when the gap between what America professes as a nation and how America behaves makes me pessimistic. I will not stop wanting America to "live up to its creed," as Martin Luther King, Jr. said. I will not stop studying the steps that the United States has taken in the region now plagued by ISIS/ISIL, nor will I ignore the missteps taken by Europe and the United States in the Middle East that have been a major cause of those groups' ruthlessness. Yet, this country, in its relatively short history, has done something both right and virtuous in extending this simplest of greetings to Marwan and so many others—"Welcome home."

The Boston Marathon Bombers and the Power of Faith

Spiritual friendships do not follow preconceived guidelines. Perhaps every friendship, spiritual or otherwise, establishes its own ground rules as it proceeds. Early in our friendship Marwan Wafa and I had to decide how we would discuss acts of violence done in the name of God. To ignore developments in the world—the civil war in Syria, the lightning growth of ISIS/ISIL, the ongoing crisis in Palestine—seemed not only unrealistic but also immoral. For a religion to be relevant, it must address the immense suffering in the world. However, an opposite danger threatens spiritual friendships; they can be derailed by crises, with conversations between partners becoming a mutual hand-wringing.

My second meeting with Marwan fell on the day after the 2013 Boston Marathon bombing. As we began to sift through our feelings about that calamity and our questions about who might be responsible, I did not know if we would or should talk about anything else. I began by sharing something I had overheard the previous evening, soon after the news about Boston began to circulate. A man in front of me in the checkout line of a supermarket looked past me to say to another man, "Well, they hit us again." That was followed by this comment: "We need to go over there and turn that whole country into a parking lot and build a Walmart." I assumed that the unnamed country the man was referring to was Iraq, Afghanistan, or Pakistan. I felt an immediate pressure to say something, anything that would make it clear that I did not share his thirst for revenge. But before I could say anything, the other man replied, "We should turn the whole place into one big lake." I imagined Marwan standing in my place in the supermarket line. Would his presence have tempered or heightened the anger of these two men? I turned to the man who had initiated the tirade and asked: "Does that mean that they've identified the country that's responsible?"

"Well, no," the first man admitted. After that an awkward, maybe a necessarily awkward, silence set in.

My anecdote saddened Marwan, but did not surprise him. Why was it so easy, he asked, for someone to blame an entire nation for the act of a misguided individual or group? He described an experience from fifteen years before, when police called to inform him that a previous neighbor had been arrested for firing a gun at the White House. Marwan's own conclusion was that the man, because of the recent death of his father, had suffered a mental collapse. "He was on the edge, a sweet guy and all that, [yet] he went and shot at the White House. So do you go wipe out {the southern Indiana town} where he lived?... So what kind of thinking do we have [here]?" In the days following our conversation, when the culprits were identified as the Tsarnaev brothers, originally from Chechnya, I recalled Marwan's final comment. "Go after the criminals," he said. "I don't care what religion or ethnic background—they did it, nail them."

Does Marwan care any less about justice in Boston, I wondered, than the two men in the supermarket? No, but what different responses. Marwan wanted the perpetrators found and punished. The other two men suggested that an entire region pay for what two hate-filled brothers had caused.

The same temptation faces us with the rise of ISIS/ISIL. One of my friends, a Muslim, is often in tears when I see her or when she communicates with me. Her tears, she explains, are for the violence being done by extremists to innocent people in Iraq and Syria, but also to Muslims whose desire is simply to live in the West, to practice their faith, and contribute to a more compassionate world. The Tsarnaev brothers misused Islam to express their pain and rage. Unfortunately, those same emotions were mirrored in the two men whom I'd overheard in the grocery store. They too were turning their rage on a region and a religion they knew little about.

As people of faith, Marwan and I needed to discuss this question: "What is the true purpose and power of religious faith?" Even as I asked Marwan to share how his Islamic faith inspired him to live with compassion, I still felt the shadow of the Tsarnaev brothers in the room. Although they did not act out of purely religious motives, their ethnic and religious background reinforced prejudices like those that Frank Laubach had noted in himself. And, as I write these words, I feel the shadow of ISIS/ISIL and other extremist groups. Why do some people feel driven, even believe called, to kill in the name of a religion that inspires others to live compassionately?

"I see me getting up early, taking a shower, coming to work and trying to change the lives of many people here as my mission," Marwan replied. "That's my mission, to help others have a better life. It is a process [students] have to go through [and, as the academic dean], I am in charge of that process. I want to make sure the process continually improves, to help them bring that change... That's my role." Marwan described how people who come into his office often apologize for bothering him. In response, he would always say, "Listen, I'm here to serve you. You're giving me a chance to serve you. Don't take that away from me." Those words made me understand what had motivated Marwan to enter into our spiritual friendship. I had imagined that he agreed at least partially out of his desire to contribute to this book. Instead, Marwan saw my request as an opportunity to serve, as part of his mission in life. "I need to serve people for me to come at the end of the day and, say, 'If I meet my Creator tonight, I feel good in the sense that I did what I could.' "

"Many times, some members of [my extended] family criticize me in the sense that [I could] make a lot more money if [I went] into business on [my] own," Marwan continued. "I get self-satisfaction helping other people stand on their feet and continue the journey. To me, this is priceless. To me, that sweaty hand when…[students] graduate, when they squeeze me or they hug me, you can't put any dollar amount [on that]."

Our second meeting made me realize that for spiritual friendships to grow, the participants must find common ground. It may appear that Marwan and I share common ground in our higher education careers. But more important than our careers is our common sense of mission, a mission rooted in our faith traditions. We both feel called to serve students, and in doing so to serve God.

In that moment of recognition, I also grasped what extremists of any religion fail to understand. It would not matter to our students that Marwan is Muslim and I am Christian. Nothing Marwan said about his joy of serving through higher education was foreign to me, for both of our faith traditions call us away from self-centeredness toward love of God and others.

Consider the example of a shy first-generation college student, uncertain if she has the intellectual abilities to succeed. No one in her family has attended college, and the fear of failure and disappointing them is strong. Yet into this anxious student's life comes a supportive faculty member who listens and offers encouragement. She not only graduates but has gained the confidence to apply for admission to the Peace Corps, or to medical school. Does it really matter to that student if her encouragement came from a Muslim, Christian, Sikh, Buddhist, or Jew? And is the benefit to the world from this student's plan to serve humanity affected by the religious identity of the person who first saw promise in her?

In subsequent months of talking with Muslims, I realized that this sense of mission that Marwan and I share is not unique. In many other areas, such as parenting, civic life, and care of the neediest, persons of faith would respond in similar if not identical ways. Yes, Muslims and Christians clearly differ in theology and worship, but concerning ethics they agree remarkably. It is important to stress our common moral principles, especially when misinformation abounds about religions. What is necessary to make the world more compassionate, more forgiving? Will interfaith dialogues between scholars or clergy bring this about? Probably not, as such dialogues tend to center on theology and often fixate on the differences. But in spiritual friendships, laypeople often find considerable agreement about how to live out our respective faiths. The survival of the human race depends on people of different faiths living out the attitude toward the neighbor expressed in the Golden Rule—"do unto others as you would have them do unto you."

Taste the Fruit

"Outcome assessment," a buzzword in higher education, resembles the biblical adage "you shall know a tree by its fruit." Religious extremism produces strong, bitter fruit, full of ruthlessness and revenge.

The fruit of spiritual friendships also has a strong taste, but it is sweet. In our friendship Marwan did not become less Muslim, nor did I become less Christian.

Neither of us embraces religious relativism or bland tolerance, and no competition to convert one another was at play in our times together. We encouraged one another to live lives of compassion and what we will later call God-centeredness or reality-centeredness. This "third way" is being experienced by a growing number of Muslims, Christians, Jews, Sikhs, Buddhists, Hindus, and people of other faiths. This path leads to religious peace and encouragement. Through spiritual friendships, the world can be changed one relationship at a time.

> No emotions are necessary. Just the doing of God's will perfectly makes the hour a perfect one. And the results of that one perfect hour, I believe, will echo down through eternity.[13]

THE PURSUIT OF GOD-CONSCIOUSNESS

In reading the Qur'an, I did not intend to ignore problematic passages that can be construed as anti-Christian and anti-Jewish. Nevertheless, spiritual friendships between Muslims and Christians focus instead on passages from our respective scriptures that encourage us to participate in the healing of the world. Debate on important theological differences should be left for scholars. Partners in spiritual friendships know from experience, however, that healing the world does not depend on scholarship. Our world, suffering from religious suspicion and violence, cannot and need not wait for intellectual consensus.

In fact, Christians who wish to develop spiritual friendships with Muslims need not read the Qur'an and the Hadiths (stories about the Prophet Muhammad and his early followers). However, given that many Muslims know portions of the Hebrew Bible (Old Testament) and the New Testament, by seeking a basic familiarity with the Qur'an, Christians or those of other faiths show respect for their Muslim friends. Furthermore, as the following pages will reveal, I have experienced something extraordinary: reading the Qur'an and Hadiths has deepened my Christian faith. What follows is a summary of the main themes of the Qur'an from which I as a Christian have profited.

The Frequency and Consequences of Unbelief

Perhaps the Qur'an's clearest message is its warning against unbelief. Unbelievers are those who deny God, God's control over history, God's grace in sending prophets to humanity, the Last Judgment, or the afterlife. Jewish and Christian texts contain obvious parallels, but the Qur'an presents a more nuanced understanding of unbelief. Unbelief is not restricted to denying the creeds of one's faith. Rather, unbelief extends as well to religious persons in those moments when they forget God, when they live lives of ingratitude and self-sufficiency.

> Among them are men who made a covenant with Allah, that if He bestowed on them of His bounty, they would give (largely) in charity, and be truly among those who are righteous. But when He did bestow of His bounty, they became covetous, and turned back (from their covenant), averse (from its fulfillment). So He has put as a consequence hypocrisy in their hearts, (to last) till the Day, whereupon they shall meet Him: because they broke their covenant with Allah, and because they lied (again and again). Know they not that Allah does know their secret (thoughts) and their counsels, and that Allah knows all things unseen? (Sura 9:75-77)

For Muslims, this is the irony of human unbelief. Although human beings forget God, a failing in which all of us are often guilty, God deserves the opposite: constant remembrance, worship, and praise. As both Bible and Qur'an repeatedly assert, God is Creator and Sustainer of all that is, seen and unseen. The very breath we are taking this moment is by the grace of God.

The Nearness of Forgiveness

A God of supreme majesty, worthy of constant praise, paired with human beings free to forget God—this combination would be deadly were it not for the assurance that God is always ready to forgive.

> If anyone does evil or wrongs his own soul but afterwards seeks Allah's forgiveness, he will find Allah Oft-Forgetting, Most Merciful. (Sura 4:110)
>
> He is the One Who accepts repentance from His servants and forgives sins: and He knows all that you do. (Sura 42:25)

God's compassion and willingness to forgive is, of course, the central hope in Judaism and Christianity. In this sense, Judaism, Christianity, and Islam are not just "Abrahamic religions" that honor a common forefather, but also *religions devoted to the Supreme and Forgiving God.* All three therefore are religions of grace, each revealing a God of mercy who offers a path to wholeness through repentance.

> Say: "O my servants who have transgressed against their souls! Despair not the Mercy of Allah: for Allah forgives all sins: for He is Oft-Forgiving, Most Merciful. Turn you to our Lord (in repentance) and submit to His (Will) before the chastisement comes on you: after that you shall not be helped." (Sura 39:53-54)[14]

The Wisdom of Submission

In Islam the proper response to God is submission. In fact, the word *Islam* literally means "to submit to God," a submission far more than an intellectual assent to God's existence and more than reverence offered on certain holy days and in certain "religious moments." In Islam, true spiritual wisdom is found in each of us admitting that in every moment of life we are either God-focused or God-forgetful. I find this particularly challenging, as western culture celebrates self-determination and self-fulfillment, not submission to God, as the source of success.

Islam confronts the sin of self-centeredness forcefully by requiring prayer five times a day. Judaism and Christianity are less direct, but would also agree: the failure to submit to God prevents humanity from fulfilling our purpose on earth of becoming our true selves. In putting self in the place of God we "miss the mark," to translate more precisely the Greek New Testament word for sin. Putting self in the place of God is to forget or deny that only God is God, and I am not. No wonder, as St. Augustine wrote, "Our hearts are restless until they find their rest in God," for we are born to submit to God in all things and at all times.

Submitting to God at this depth and frequency is one of the lessons that Islam has to offer Christians, especially Western Christians like myself. By devoting most of our days to a consumer culture of work, chores, sports, entertainment, and eating out, we confine God to sanctuaries that we visit once a week or where we spend a few moments before we eat or fall asleep. Islam reminds us that the God of Abraham, Moses, David, and Isaiah is not a "God of convenience."

Taqwa, *God-consciousness*

I first recall hearing the phrase "God consciousness" during my research for *Peace Be with You: Monastic Wisdom for a Terror-Filled World.* Sister Mary Margaret Funk, from Our Lady of Grace Monastery in Beech Grove, Indiana, told me that she had come to realize that faithful Muslims have an experience of God-consciousness, but too few Christians do. She suggested that instead our culture promotes "food-consciousness," "sex-consciousness," and "thing-consciousness."[15]

But Sister Meg assured me that life need not be confined to battling these competing kinds of consciousness. "You know, God's grace is very available but these afflictions are just hiding everything. [Fortunately] the monastic archetype is in every soul."[16] She maintained firmly that, with faithful Muslims, Christians can embrace God-consciousness not as yet another kind of awareness to add to the list, but as "an alternative culture."

So what does *taqwa*—God-consciousness—mean in day-to-day practice? God-consciousness is not piously thinking heavenly thoughts constantly or offering conscious prayer every moment. God-consciousness does not pull a person away from everyday activities; instead, it "re-texturizes" those activities. Can God be experienced in a work of art or at a concert? Can God be experienced in the moment of stillness felt after a brisk walk, or in the sense of closeness during a meal with close friends? Can God be present in a tense business meeting, at the deathbed of a friend, or in a traffic jam? The prophet Isaiah called God *Immanuel*, God with us. Because God is God-with-us, should we not then seek to live within that consciousness?

Lest Christians dismiss God-consciousness as solely Islamic or impossible to achieve, note the similarity between *taqwa* and the maxims of one of the early Christian Fathers of the East, Isaac of Nineveh.[17]

> Be mindful of God, so that in every moment he may be mindful of you. If he is mindful of you, he will give you salvation.
>
> Do not forget him, letting yourselves be seduced by vain distractions...
>
> Remain constantly before his face, think of him, remember him in your heart. Otherwise, if you only meet him from time to time, you risk losing your close friendship with him...
>
> Those who would see the Lord should purify their hearts with the continual remembrance of God. They will reach the contemplation of God in every moment, and within him all will be light.[18]

With God-consciousness, then, Islam is emphasizing not something foreign to Christianity, but a practice of early Christians. Contemporary Christians can regain part of our own heritage by pondering *taqwa.*

And what is the payoff of practicing this God-consciousness? Christians and Muslims who live within the consciousness of God the Creator and Sustainer experience nothing short of the miraculous transformation of secular life. Every moment becomes sanctified.

What God Has Joined Together, Let No One Put Asunder

Many people continue to ask if establishing spiritual friendships with Muslims and reading Islamic scriptures have diluted my Christian faith. Diluted? No. Deepened it? Yes. How? I spoke recently at a conservative Christian college about how my spiritual friendships with Muslims had strengthened my faith. After the class a student approached me and said, "If I understand you correctly, you are a religious pluralist." My answer surprised her. I am not a pluralist but an "inclusivist." Religious pluralists believe all religions are equally valid, while inclusivists maintain that their own faith is the clearest path of knowing God, even as they acknowledge that God can and does speak and work through other religions.

Eboo Patel, head of the Interfaith Youth Core, provided an excellent example of faith that is inclusive when he spoke at Franklin College. He surprised some in the audience when he said that he expected Christians listening to him to believe that their faith is the best of the religions, even as he believes that Islam is the best. He followed this by asserting that such devotion need not hinder the two faith traditions working together to create a more peaceful world. And Eboo Patel is entirely right.

I began my spiritual journey as an exclusivist, but in my adult years changed to a Christian inclusivist position. Put another way, I have journeyed gradually from imagining God being contained in the box of one religion—my own—to understanding that God, as God, can never be confined. Believing that Jesus is the Son of God does not mean that I deny God's working through other faith traditions. This is not simply my belief; it is also my experience. In spiritual friendships with Muslims, Jews, Sikhs, Hindus, and Buddhists, I have experienced God's love in undeniable ways. Also, my reading the scriptures of other faiths has been enriched through a similar inclusivist position. God speaks most clearly to me through the Bible, but God can and does speak through the scriptures of other faith traditions.

The following hadith, one of the stories from or about Muhammad, is a shining example of how God has spoken to me through another faith tradition. When I first read it, I realized immediately that this text was in "conversation" with one of the more important sayings of Jesus. Upon further reflection, I understood that this "conversation" offers a post-9/11 ethic that can help heal our broken world.

Hadith Sahih Muslim, Book 32, No. 6232

> Abu Huraira reported Allah's Messenger (may peace be upon him) as saying: Verily, Allah, the Exalted and Glorious, would say on the Day of Resurrection: O son of Adam, I was sick but you did not visit Me. He would say: O my Lord; how could I visit Thee whereas Thou art the Lord of the worlds? Thereupon He would say: Didn't you know that such and such servant of Mine was sick but you did not visit him and were you not aware of this that if you had visited him, you would have found Me by him? O son of Adam, I asked food from you but you did not feed Me. He would say: My Lord, how could I feed Thee whereas Thou art the Lord of the worlds? He said: Didn't you know that such and such servant of Mine asked food from you but you did not feed him, and were you not aware that if you had fed him you would have found him by My side? (The Lord would again say): O son of Adam, I asked drink from you but you did not provide Me. He would say: My Lord, how could I provide Thee whereas Thou art the Lord of the worlds? Thereupon He would say: Such and such of servant of Mine asked you for a drink but you did not provide him, and had you provided him drink you would have found him near Me.

The first lines of this hadith contain an echo of one of the most important sayings of Jesus, the warning about the Day of Judgment from Matthew 25:31-46.

> When the Son of man comes in his glory, and all the angels with him, then he will sit on his glorious throne. Before him will be gathered all the nations, and he will separate them one from another as a shepherd separates the sheep from the goats, and he will place the sheep at his right hand, but the goats at the left. Then the King will say to those at his right hand, "Come, O blessed of my Father, inherit the kingdom prepared for you from the foundation of the world; for I was hungry and you gave me food, I was thirsty and you gave me drink, I was a stranger and you welcomed me, I was naked and you clothed me, I was sick and you visited me, I was in prison and you came to me." Then the righteous will answer him "Lord, when did we see thee hungry and feed thee, or thirsty and give thee drink? And when did we see thee sick or in prison and visit thee?" And the King will answer them, "Truly I say to you, as you did it to one of the least of these my brethren, you did it to me." Then he will say to those at his left hand, "Depart from me, you cursed, into the eternal fire prepared for the devil and his angels; for I was hungry and you gave me no food, I was thirsty and you gave me no drink, I was a stranger and you did not welcome me, naked and you did not clothe me, sick and in prison and you did not visit me." Then they also will answer, "Lord when did we see thee hungry or thirsty or a stranger or naked or sick or in prison, and did not minister to thee?" Then he will answer them, "Truly I say to you, as you did it not to one of the least of these, you did it not to me." And they will go away into eternal punishment, but the righteous into eternal life. (*RSV*)

The saying of Jesus and the hadith from Muhammad direct believers of both religions to a common meeting point. In our post-9/11 age of religious suspicion and terrorism, especially with the rise of ISIS/ISIL and other extremist groups, faith communities are tempted to wall themselves off from one another. As exemplified by the parallel between the hadith and Matthew 25, I believe that God is calling Muslims and Christians to a different future, one where seeking to love God through serving those most in need brings us together for the healing of the world.

In Mark 10:9, Jesus says, "What God has joined together, let no one separate." Could this admonition apply as much to friendships, especially spiritual friendships, as to marriage? What healing could come to our sorrowful world—Syria, the West Bank and Gaza, Afghanistan, Iraq, Egypt, the Central African Republic, Yemen, Lebanon, Nigeria, and your community and mine—if people of faith believed that God is calling us to "join together" to respond to the needs of others?

LORD, TEACH US TO PRAY

> One need not tell God *everything* about the people for whom one prays. Holding them one by one steadily before the mind and willing that God may have His will with them is the best, for God knows better than we what our friends need, our prayer releases His power, we know not how.[19]

I KNEW THAT MY NEXT meeting with Marwan Wafa would be different. There had been no recent terrorist attack, such as the Boston bombing, to frame our conversation. Also, I came with a question. Could he show me how the Islamic understanding of prayer differed from the Christian understanding?

Sometimes a person realizes only in retrospect that something read or heard has brought about a fundamental change. Much rarer are those experiences when a person is fully aware of such a change as it is occurring. Marwan's answer to my question about prayer produced a "tectonic" shift in me. Forty-five minutes into our conversation, I knew that my prayer life would never be the same.

He explained the several types of prayer in Islam. In addition to the five daily prayers there are others to be said in any moment of need. Before the formal prayer they perform ablutions. Marwan compared the practice with a person meeting a celebrity, such as the president of the United States. Any person so fortunate would be clean, well-groomed, and well-dressed. "Here [in prayer] we're not talking about a person but the Creator of all things, the Master of the Day of Judgment, and you are preparing to meet with Him through the prayers. It's a meeting, a communication," he explained. The ablutions serve as a way of switching modes or spiritual states, when five times a day a person leaves one's daily routine to enter into prayer. He then shared an original insight about washing the face and head. "The head is very important. That's where the brain is. So [by washing the face] you're cooling down, which I think helps slow things down in our thinking...to where you're ready to talk with God.... The cleansing allows you to think, 'I am going to pray. I am going to meet God through prayers.' "

The Islamic practice of ablutions resembles the Christian practice of bowing, genuflecting, or making the sign of the cross before prayer. Those too are types of preparation, a centering of one's entire being into the heart and acknowledging that we are created and God is Creator. When Marwan raised an aspect of Islamic prayer that was new to me, his words spoke powerfully to my heart. "Before you even start the prayers," he said, "you have to have the intention. It is called *niyah*; *niyah* is intention." Intention relates to the motive behind any human action. As an example, he referred to something from our previous conversation. What is a person's intention when heading off for work? It is not only to make as much money as possible, but to help others and make a living in the process.

"For prayers, it is likewise," Marwan explained. "You go through the mechanics of cleansing, right, but then before you start the prayer you have to reset...with the *niyah*. 'I intend to offer You, Lord, my noon prayer, hoping that you will accept it.' And then you start the prayers." I asked Marwan to pause so I could ponder the effect of these last words. In that silence, I came face to face with a new understanding not just of prayer, but of the pinnacle of Christian prayer, the Lord's Prayer. *Your will be done on earth, as it is in heaven.* Those words kept repeating in my mind. In pondering them, I realized that I had been treating them as a mere formulaic introduction to the rest of the prayer. The later petition for daily bread, the request for forgiveness as we forgive, and the petition for protection from evil had always seemed to be the "meat" of the prayer. When Marwan spoke about checking one's *niyah*, one's intention, before prayer, however, I understood those words: *Your will be done on earth, as it is in heaven* in a new and radical way. In that moment, the phrase did not seem a mere introduction, but the most important words, words that established the proper intention for the remainder of the Lord's Prayer.

It is easy to assume that prayer is always good. Martin Luther, however, knew better. He noted that prayer can be an occasion for tremendous sin. If we come to God with our hearts and minds dominated by self-centeredness, we will pray selfishly, as the Pharisee does in the parable in Luke 18:9-14. God must hear many prayers that ask Him to shower the petitioner with blessings of health or success. Marwan's words opened up the meaning of "*Your will be done on earth, as it is in heaven.*" Jesus was encouraging his disciples, before asking God for anything, to relinquish their own wills. And then I realized that *niyah,* or proper intention, was precisely what Jesus offered in the Garden of Gethsemane, when He concluded His plea to be spared the cross with the words "Yet, not my will but Yours be done." I wondered, is this not also a "Lord's Prayer," something that I, as a disciple of Jesus, need to pray in that same way, in that same spirit?

After our conversation I realized that Marwan's explanation would change more than how I prayed the Lord's Prayer. Those simple words "Your will be done" must be the way that God wishes us to begin all prayer.

Rolling the Credits

Uttering spontaneous prayers whenever necessary is certainly not wrong. But to pause before prayer, to reflect on the intention of my heart and to reflect on God's majestic Otherness and Godness, is also necessary.

From my filmmaker son, I have learned that nothing so exasperates a director as an arrogant actor who refuses to take direction, who believes that he or she has a better grasp of what the character being portrayed should do or say. In those moments, such actors are actually "sinning against the director," forgetting that it is not the actors but the director who determines how a scene should play out and what the actors should say and do to be true to their characters.

To say before prayer with our whole heart "Your will be done on earth/in my life as it is in heaven" is to acknowledge that we are in the presence of God, the one who has a clear vision of the unfolding scenes of our lives and the lives of everyone around us. In prayer, we bring to God our concerns, our fears, our hopes, our joys, knowing that we understand only partially the present scene or chapter of the story of which we are but a part.

That day's conversation with Marwan has continued to convict and challenge me. How often have I gone to God in prayer and asked Him to bless the plan that I have in mind or, even worse, the plan that I have already set in motion? Too often, I have communicated with God as if I am the director of my life story and God is the producer, the one who is supposed to bankroll my story. Through Marwan, I am learning to pray in a different way, not by *ending* my prayer with a throwaway line of "in Jesus' name" or "may your will be done," but by *beginning* my prayer attending to *niyah,* my heart's intention, by consciously pausing to ask that God's will, not mine, be done.

Truly, that is the way to pray *in Jesus' name.*

PART II:
THE SHAPIRO GANG

A DREAM UNEXPECTEDLY FULFILLED

Over twenty years ago, I dreamed that I was sitting at a long table overflowing with food. Marble walls and floors gave the hall a medieval feeling. My place at the table was halfway down one side, and from that vantage point I could not see who is sitting at the head. But I was aware that other men occupied every seat.

The most powerful aspect of the dream was not the richness of the décor or the abundance of food, but rather the joy that flowed among those gathered around the table. No one was trying to "one-up" anyone else in the easy-flowing and quite boisterous conversation. The bond that I had with these "dream friends" suggested that we all knew each other too well and cared about one another too much to engage in petty competitiveness. The dream had no sequence of events that made up a plot, so its feeling remained memorable. As I shared the dream with a therapist-friend, I realized that I understood the dream's meaning. I had dreamt about the quality of relationships with men that I wished to have, but had not been able to achieve. The wise therapist asked me to stay with the dream, saying that I needed to work not on the visual details but the sadness with which the dream had left me. At the time I did not realize that the dream is spiritual. Nor did I realize that my longing is not unique to me. Thousands of men in our culture share a similar dream.

Over the years much of the sadness of the dream has dissipated. I have been blessed with friendships with Tim, Taso, George, Jim, John, Gordon, Tony, Frank, David, Steve, Angelo, and many others, including some of the monks whom I interviewed for *Peace Be with You: Monastic Wisdom for a Terror-Filled World*. Although I developed a separate friendship with each of these men, I had never found the key to that room where a circle of men was waiting for me.

But in 2012 I found that key when I began to meet with Christian and Muslim men at Shapiro's Deli in downtown Indianapolis. The longer that I meet with these very common yet uncommon men, the more I sensed the fulfillment of my dream. Shapiro's Deli does not have marble walls, and the table does not overflow with food, but there I found the camaraderie I had been seeking.

John Mundell, one of the group's founding members, described the bond linking the men this way: "There is this presence of God [here], and each experiences that. And it has transformed us individually and collectively." John Welch, the senior member of the group, agrees. "One of the things that I feel very strongly is that God reveals Himself to us in this relationship…This relationship is different and it is quite amazing."

Common Men, Uncommon Group

When he invited me to join the group at Shapiro's, John Welch did not hide the fact that the group identifies with the Focolare. At the time, I knew little about this movement, and the Shapiro's group of Muslim and Christian men remains my only experience of the Focolare. I decided at the outset that I would let the Shapiro group define itself. I would base my assessment by the members' treatment of one another and me, even though I knew that the Focolare has its critics.

When I began to attend, I observed that the group follows no set procedure. Once a month, John Welch brings a small two-sided sheet of paper that sets forth a simple biblical phrase for the month along with a short devotional. But in our weekly meetings over the next two years, this monthly tract usually played a minimal part in our discussion. In fact, my recordings of the lunches reveal that the group followed no script at all. There is not even a prayer said aloud to begin the gatherings. At the Wednesday lunches the men discuss whatever is on their minds. I also observed the composition of the group to be quite fluid. There is never any pressure to attend, nor is the return of anyone after a significant absence ever mentioned. Later, I concluded that what held the group together is not organizational commitment, attendance policy, or curriculum, but their mutual esteem and love.

I noticed immediately that these men were extremely comfortable with one another. They do not fear to confront any subject, religious or otherwise. And while I initially expected the Muslims to be closer to the other Muslims and likewise for the Christians, the reality of the Shapiro group is much different. There are no religious cliques that I can perceive. If anything, their relationships across religious lines seem as strong as, or stronger than, those within the participating religious groups.

Of course, it was not long before the uncommonness of these lunches piqued my curiosity about the Focolare Movement's origins. John Welch gave me a used copy of a biography of the movement's founder, and the book deepened my appreciation for the spiritual friendships that exist between these Muslim and Christian men. I have concluded that the "Shapiro gang" is the healthiest group of spiritual men that I have ever known. Over time I discovered that an important clue to the nature of their bond is as much what these very common men *don't* talk about as what they *do*.

Rethinking Sports

Imagine a popular deli only blocks from two massive sports arenas: Lucas Oil Stadium, where the Indianapolis Colts play, and Bankers Life Fieldhouse, where the Indiana Pacers play. Sports posters cover the walls. The napkin dispensers on every table list the home games of the local team, basketball or football depending on the season. At most lunchtimes, at Shapiro's Deli men outnumber women four to one, sometimes closer to ten to one.

Not until the week when the Indiana Pacers took the Miami Heat to the seventh game in the 2013 playoffs did one jarring fact dawn on me. The Focolare table was having its usual Wednesday lunch when a young man came in carrying a "Beat the Heat" poster. At that moment, as I glanced around the packed deli, I realized that I had never talked about sports with these men. How is that possible, I thought? How is it that a group of American men, gathering weekly at a deli in the shadow of two massive sports facilities, has never reverted to what must be the default topic of most male gatherings anywhere in the United States? The table of Focolare men must be the only one there that does not rely on sports to grease the conversation.

I pointed to the young man carrying the poster and offered a prediction to the other men at the table. "I bet if I had a nickel for every conversation going on in this deli today that is sports-related, I'd be a pretty rich man at the end of the day." I also acknowledged that I would be flat-broke if I relied on the Focolare group to contribute to those same funds. As I shared my observation, the men seemed unaware of what to me seemed to be a significant characteristic of their gatherings. My observation had obviously surprised them.

John broke the silence. "If you love everyone, you love the other team," he said with one of his characteristic shrugs. Picking up the thread of John's comment, Joe, the youngest member of the group, added that there is a great deal of aggression in talking about sports as well as a tendency to bond around the teams you and your friends hate. I could not help but reflect that the poster "Beat the Heat" never even mentioned the Pacers. Aggressiveness and hate, Joe concluded, are not the values encouraged by the Focolare.

Encouraged by Joe's observation, I shared a change that had occurred in me after 9/11. If I focused on what humanity needs to do to heal the world, I could no longer watch hour after hour of sports on TV. This change came about because of my increasing discomfort with the desire of teams and individual athletes not only to win but to dominate, even obliterate, the opponent. Taken together, the exorbitant salaries, the celebratory dances in the end zone after a touchdown, the he-man grimacing after a slam dunk resemble the actions of Roman gladiators. I shared that professional sport seemed not just a distraction from what we needed to focus on—poverty, hunger, demonization of the "other"—but, given the money and time devoted to watching professional sports, a form of cultural idolatry. I explained that I have no problem with sport as an activity, emphasizing the word "active," or even the occasional enjoyment of watching sport performed at a high level, but what does it say about contemporary culture, I posed, that it offers numerous cable channels devoted to round-the-clock sports coverage?

I had never admitted this to any other man. I also realized that what I had admitted would likely make no sense to any of the other tables of men in Shapiro's that day; the guy with the "Beat the Heat" poster would probably laugh at me. But no one at this table of uncommon men laughed at or ridiculed me.

Honoring Women

The "ball and chain," the "little lady," the "boss," the "battleax," "she who must be obeyed." Over the years I have been with other men and I have heard women referred to with such words or phrases—or others not so nice. Much as with sports, male conversation, especially when alcohol is involved, often descends to denigrating women. Certainly no one at our table ever suggested "women" as a topic for conversation. Yet, over the months of meeting with these men, I noticed that they consistently speak lovingly, appreciatively, and naturally of their wives. In several lunchtime conversations, one or more of the men shared a memory of a picnic they had had the previous summer, when they had invited their entire families, particularly their wives. The men told me that over the years, their wives had expressed the desire to meet the other men of the group who have had such a profound influence on their husbands.

It was John Welch who demonstrated how their attitude toward women differs from what might be expressed in conventional male conversation. After I had met with the group for several months, John asked me when the group could meet "your lovely bride." It was also John who, after sharing that his wife suffers from tremors, added, "So I do all the cooking." After a pause, he added, "I'm happy." And his face indicated that that is the truth.

Knowing that Islamic men are often accused of harboring attitudes that belittle women, I was interested in what David or Mikal, the main Muslim members, might say. I had seen a YouTube video of Mikal and his wife speaking on marriage at a regional Focolare gathering, and it was clear that she does not live in her husband's shadow. I was also impressed when John shared that a Muslim man had once told him his relationship to his wife was to "protect her," and David Shaheed commented that a man does not protect his wife as he would a child but as an equal.

Where's the Barking Dog?

A third uncommon and surprising characteristic of the group is the absence of an "alpha dog." Who is the leader here? Whose dominance or weighted silence indicates a right of primacy among the group? Who among the men asserts his point of view as the correct one, the one that demands the respect of the others? John has seniority by age, but it would be unfair to call him the group's lead dog. To my amazement, none of the men fills this role. How is it, I wondered, that this group of men has managed to achieve equity?

The group is clearly an uncommon "association of men." So what, instead of sports, macho attitudes toward women, or the establishing of an alpha dog accounts for these welcome peculiarities? The best way to describe this other focus is that each man in the group understands himself and the other men as sharing in a common adventure with God. A key part of that adventure is being with one another in an alternative cultural way where, instead of competing or engaging in small talk, they encourage one another to embrace this journey and they forgive one another when they fail.

I have concluded that this focus, this form of God-consciousness, is the key to their life together. These men do not despise sports, but something in their lives clearly interests them more. I suspect that these men indeed have had disagreements with their spouses and rough patches in their marriages. But once again, another preoccupation—seeking the will of God in the present moment—must have brought them back into realignment with their spouses after egotism had temporarily gained the upper hand.

And even more clearly, their God-consciousness explains the lack of a pecking order among them. They do not compete with one another; rather, they share this adventure together. Their masculine aggression had been channeled into living as "spiritual explorers," explorers of the inner life. Each of them is living out his life challenges in his own unique way, but together they have the adventure in common. Perhaps, in the end, the "alpha dog" of the Shapiro group is the One Who calls them daily as Muslims and Christians to continue on the journey of faith.

Reflecting on these men, the Shapiro group reminded me of Dietrich Bonhoeffer's underground community during the Third Reich, described in his book *Life Together.* As it was with Jesus' disciples and Muhammad's first followers, the government paid no attention to Bonhoeffer's group. Yet, Bonhoeffer and the fellow members of his underground community were the righteous remnant that saved the soul of Germany. I see this group in a similar light. It is unlikely that the Indianapolis media outlets will feature these men in the news. Yet without fanfare together these ordinary men are living out an adventure with God. Because of their shared commitment, they are healing the brokenness of the world.

After meeting with the men for four or five months, I shared another conviction that had been growing stronger in me. When I sit at the table with these Muslims and Christians, I feel that I am tasting the future of the world. The natural way they share their lives of faith seems a foretaste of what the world could become. In response to my enthusiasm John Welch offered one of his characteristic shrugs. What they have together is "a *possible* future of the world," he said. John is right. Followers of the major world religions can choose to build walls rather than bridges. Even if spiritual friendships are the will of God, as I believe they are, they are only a possible future. People of diverse faiths will have to take the courageous step of sitting across from one another at tables in delis, work lunchrooms, and homes to talk about how their faith shapes their lives.

Nevertheless, if these ordinary men, who for over nineteen years have been meeting at Shapiro's, are able to encourage one another on their adventure with God, why can't similar groups form across this country and the world?

MUSLIMS AND CHRISTIANS ON AN ADVENTURE WITH GOD

THE SHAPIRO MEN AVOID the spotlight. Undoubtedly, they would tell me that they are the most ordinary of people. In one sense, they are right; but, in another, I am convinced that they are anything but ordinary. That is not just my opinion. Speaking throughout the country about spiritual friendships and sharing my experiences with Muslims, I have been asked repeatedly about these men, especially how they began meeting together.

That story begins in 1995 when Chiara Lubich, the female, Christian, Italian founder of the Focolare, began a life-changing friendship with the male, black, Muslim son of Elijah Muhammad, Imam W.D. Muhammad, the person most responsible for bringing many in his father's Nation of Islam into conformity with normative Sunni Islam. The Shapiro men and many others consider the unexpected friendship of these two leaders a miracle and a blessing.

From 1995 to 1999, an amazing relationship blossomed between these two very different partners. Earlier Chiara Lubich had seen that the charism of the Focolare included non-Christians. In an address to 12,000 Buddhist leaders, Chiara Lubich expressed the movement's simple spiritual guideline in this way: "The heart of my experience is this: the more we love the other, the more we find God. The more we find God, the more we love others." [20] In 1995 Cardinal William Keeler of Baltimore introduced Chiara Lubich and W.D. Muhammad to one another. By 1997, the friendship had deepened, as demonstrated by Imam Muhammad's invitation for Lubich to speak to the Muslim community assembled at Malcolm Shabazz Mosque in New York. Her remarks included this startling observation:

> I feel very much at home with Imam Mohammed, as I do with other leaders. Actually, I feel even more at home with Imam Mohammed because I think that the Lord has brought him especially close to us, just as the Lord brought us close to him, perhaps because of a plan of love that we will understand as we continue to collaborate and work together.[21]

In his gracious response, the imam said:

> So this idea that is in the Focolare is something that our soul knows and wants, and for that reason I have embraced them as my friends and I admire them greatly and I believe in their movement, and I consider myself a person who is open to their influence.[22]

Their friendship deepened as the two leaders traveled together to Rome to meet Pope John Paul II. There, Imam W.D. Mohammed asked the pope to bless this "beautiful working relationship...so we can have a better world for all."[23]

In the wake of this cordial beginning, both leaders gave similar instructions to their flocks: Muslims and Christians need to know one another. With that mission in mind, in 1996 Focolare leaders from Chicago travelled to Indianapolis to meet local Muslim and Christian leaders. At that encounter John Welch and Mikal Saahir met. Both Christians and Muslims welcomed the meeting enthusiastically. And it was then, after this first meeting, that the group retreated to Shapiro's Deli. After the Chicago representatives departed, John Welch and Mikal Saahir both remember asking themselves the same question: "What now?" Not knowing how to proceed, they agreed to return the next week to Shapiro's. These men have been meeting together there ever since.

When Welch asked the Focolare leaders from Chicago for advice about the Indianapolis group's agenda, they told him: "Put duct tape over your mouth." Mikal Saahir also received advice, in his case from Imam W.D. Muhammad himself. When he inquired what Muslims should be learning from the Focolare, Imam Muhammad, to Mikal's surprise—and mine—replied, "to practice Christ's love." Instead of talking theology, these men understood their mission as encouraging each other to live the word of God, as they found it in the Qur'an and the Bible. They shared a common understanding that living the word of God means loving one another, not converting each other.

Mikal shared how outsiders have difficulty understanding this shared goal. He recalled a Muslim friend who stopped by the group's table, asking Mikal what their gathering was about. When Mikal explained how the group comprised Muslims and Catholics, the man "pulled up his seat [and declared], 'All right; let's get it on.'" Mikal explained that they came together as family, not foes, but the man would not believe him. "I think he was let down when he went home," Mikal said with a smile.

The Most Difficult "Simple" Challenge in the World

These men exemplify how Muslims and Christians can be spiritual friends. Although they are not afraid to share their beliefs freely and naturally, they seek not to resolve theological differences but to encourage one another. When I asked one of the Catholic men if the Muslim members had ever encouraged him to read the Qur'an, he looked puzzled by the question. The absence of debate, however, does not mean that the men's table conversation is a series of pious phrases. The men truly love one another as family, but that love is not a sentiment or feeling. Rather, their love is an action, seen specifically in their commitment to come together every week as brothers.

What the men do invites a reconception of what "faith" means. Some Christians and Muslims might define their belief as a set of doctrines or creedal statements. But for the Shapiro men faith is far simpler. As John Welch noted at one of the lunches, "Chiara Lubich always said that God only asks something very simple of us. We are to do the will of God in the present moment." What God asks might have seemed simple to Lubich, but most people—including me— find that attending to the will of God is easier said than done.

Those who know me would say that I am considerate of the feelings of others, happy to befriend strangers, a good team player. As a workshop leader, I am skilled in mediating conflict and facilitating others' learning. Those very attributes lead most people to affirm me and my contributions. As the world sees me, I appear to be one nice guy. Much of my "niceness," to tell the truth, is rooted not in my Christian faith, but in my Scandinavian heritage. Generally, we are a careful don't-make-a-fuss people, adept at skillful bobbing, weaving, and slipping verbal traps to avoid alienating others. Jesus warned his followers that it would be better to cut off an offending limb or remove an eye than forfeit the Kingdom of God. The application to my own life is clear. I would be better off if I were less Scandinavian, less skilled at projecting a concern for others while being primarily intent on protecting myself. That I have learned to take care of myself by schmoozing rather than by cursing or brawling, as my Viking ancestors did, does not make me any better in God's view.

This type of self-reflection or soul-searching has come to me more frequently and naturally after spending time with the group. Through them, I have come to see that the "simple" faith that Chiara Lubich taught and lived out is profoundly challenging. I suspect that I am not alone in admitting this.

Hope Trumps Zeal

Living the will of God in every moment is a brilliantly inclusive ethic, a calling central to Islam, Judaism, Hinduism, and Sikhism as it is to Christianity. Even many Buddhists who may not believe in a god nevertheless are able to embrace the spirit of living the will of God. Of course, Christian, Jewish, and Islamic extremist groups can interpret the goal of doing the will of God in the present moment to mean defending their faith against "others." Al-Qaeda, the Tsarnaev brothers, ISIS/ISIL, and extremist groups in the West might validate their messages of hate and acts of terror by claiming to be doing the will of God in the present moment.

Among these men, I find the dynamic driving force of the group to be *hope* rather than *zeal.* These men are living out a hope that they understand as God's dream for the world, a hope that leads them to build bridges. Once again, these men would admit only that they are ordinary persons committed to this unusual adventure with God. They are ordinary in many ways. Even their spiritual practice, as I have witnessed it, seems ordinary on the surface. Yet, to be in their presence and feel their connection as brothers is to be within something powerful, something that they believe God wishes to offer to everyone.

Recovering the Penance in Penitentiary

While interviewing monks and nuns for *Peace Be with You: Monastic Wisdom for a Terror-Filled World,* I kept imagining how different the lives of juvenile first offenders would be if they were not sent to detention facilities, but to monasteries. In lockups, young men and women experience change, but quite often a negative change as they receive what often turns out to be a higher education in crime. In monasteries, the spiritual wisdom of monks and nuns could not help but have the opposite effect, a transforming one.

I have a similar conviction about the effect of the Shapiro group. Young men could hardly do better than to have such guides as mentors. Even though I am no longer young, I have felt their collective faith working on me, drawing me closer to a God who wishes me to live the holy adventure. The following profiles exemplify what I previously discovered in my interviews with monks and nuns—their common sense of the adventure with God has heightened, rather than obscured, each person's distinctiveness. Their example challenges me not to become a copy of anyone, but rather to become the person that God has always intended me to be.

John Welch

Well into his eighties, John until recently worked as the CEO and founder of an Indianapolis violin-making firm. And even though this Catholic layman does not attempt to lead the group, he is its senior member. A gifted storyteller, he seasons his anecdotes with humor, an infectious smile, a shrug, and, most tellingly, a childlike sense of what might be termed "spiritual wonder." In his younger days a jazz trombonist who played with the likes of Charlie Parker, John remains an entertainer, a dapper dresser, a charmer, a man gifted in bringing people together.

The story of how a jazz musician from New York City ended up in Indiana is interwoven with John's attachment to the Focolare. He recalls how he and his wife were invited to hear one of the leaders of the Focolare in North America. "She [the speaker] just wiped me out," John explained. But his wife, Mary, whom he describes as coming from German and English stock, "doesn't jump into anything." In the car after hearing the speaker, however, Mary said to John, "About this [the Focolare] I have no reservations."

Shortly thereafter, John had lunch with another leader of the Focolare. He remembers the man encouraging him to be open to what God wanted to do with him. That comment had a life-changing effect on John when, at almost the same time, he received a job offer from a friend who had started a publishing business in Lebanon, Indiana, a small town north of Indianapolis. Given Mary's and his love of New York City, the decision seemed easy. He called his friend in Indiana and declined the offer. Soon after, Mary and he shared their feelings about the decision. "She looked at me and said, 'this doesn't feel right.' And I said, 'Me neither.'" John picked up the phone, called the friend back in Indiana, and said, "We're coming." That decision brought the Welches to central Indiana in the 1960s. Once there, they began to share with other couples their Focolare experience of "trying to live [the will of God]."

Many of John's stories concern God's asking him to set aside his practicality. Such surrender seems to lie at the heart of his adventure with God. Because "Islam" means submission to God, I was not surprised that John's stories have struck a responsive chord with the Muslim men in the group. In one of his stories, John describes being on his way to Dallas for business. He prefers to begin his day by attending Mass because, he often says with a smile, "I need all the help I can get." The sign at the Catholic church in the town he was passing through indicated that Mass would not be until five that afternoon. The sensible thing to do, John thought to himself, was to head for Dallas where he would almost certainly find a church with an evening Mass. But what John likes to call the "little voice" told him to go to the rectory and ask the priest for the Eucharist—in extraordinary circumstances, Catholics can request to receive communion outside of the celebration of the Mass. Sacred hosts are reserved in the tabernacle for such purposes. "I finally gave in," he said, adding that ringing the doorbell early in the morning was "like sticking my finger in a light socket." The priest who came to the door agreed to his request.

As they walked through the narthex of the church, John was surprised to see a diocesan newspaper with the face of Chiara Lubich on the cover. The priest, who later confessed to not knowing much about the Focolare, seemed interested that John knew a great deal about who the woman was. After offering John communion, the priest shared that a group of women would be meeting with him that morning. Would John be willing to postpone leaving for Dallas and speak to the group? Despite his tight schedule, John agreed. He told the women of the Focolare spirituality, which encourages people to pursue the will of God on a daily basis. Their enthusiasm, John shared, was "like popcorn going off."

Several women asked when he would be stopping through their town again. He answered, "I may never come back through here," but added that in the trunk of his car he had a magazine with more information about Chiara Lubich and the Focolare. As he offered the magazine, John realized that the priest was crying. The pastor admitted that he had been considering leaving the priesthood. "He said, 'I was so down, and then you came and rang my bell.' "

And there the story ended, leaving me to wrestle with John's conviction that a "little voice" had led him to set aside his own desire. Growing up in a Baptist parsonage, quite early I became cynical of people who said they knew the will of God. Often, I noticed, the "will of God" turned out to be a justification of what the person had already set his or her heart on. But the more I thought about what John had shared, the more I realized that what he did was the opposite of my cynical experience. It was not a case of baptizing his own wishes in "God talk," but a case of doing something that seemed contrary to his reasoning mind. I thought how easy it would have been for John to dismiss that inner nudge, to veto that voice on practical grounds—"I have all these things on my plate today"; "I've already made business appointments in Dallas"; or "I will be imposing on this parish priest who, if he's like most priests in the United States, is already overburdened." How easy it would have been to rationalize his way right out of town. After a few moments of reflection, I shared my admiration of how in that situation John was able to relinquish control. He nodded then said that he understood very well the temptation to control matters. That led him to tell another story, one that would hold up a mirror to my own life.

Once while in Copenhagen on business, John found a restaurant near his hotel. As soon as he sat down at a table, he was surprised to find two Danish couples leaving their table to sit down next to him. "It wasn't in a friendly way," John explained. "They had a real live American, and they were really going to do their thing. So they were very aggressive, [saying] 'you believe this; you believe that.' They were very anti-American." As John told his story, my thoughts drifted back to my graduate school days in Scotland during the last years of the Vietnam conflict, when without warning my wife and I could be cornered by Brits, friends or strangers, who wanted us to "explain" American foreign policy. I remembered far too well how the conversations became tense and then tenser. Those were some of the few times when my Scandinavian ability to deflect did not work. Even when Kathy and I stated that we did not support the Vietnam conflict, we were still treated as stand-ins for the Nixon administration. I was so lost in this memory that at first I did not hear what John said next about his own experience in Copenhagen. "The whole thing started to warm up, and by the end of the evening, they walked me back to my hotel," he said softly. "They said, 'if you ever come back, don't stay in a hotel; stay with us.'" Even when John repeated his words, I was confused. Clearly, my own memory of being treated as an "ugly American" had caused me to miss what had so transformed the Danish couples.

"What do you think melted them?" I asked

John offered his characteristic shrug again before repeating a phrase from St. John of the Cross. "Where there is no love, put love, and you will find love."

I still did not understand. In comparison with my own similar experience, I could not connect the story's beginning and its end. Somehow John had found a different way of avoiding the defensiveness and acid aftertaste of resentment that had typified much of my experience while living abroad in the early 1970s. John's story, however, is not about what he had managed to avoid. Rather, it was about the love that had arisen.

Months later and six hundred miles away, standing on a barren hillside in Omaha, Nebraska, I managed to understand what must have happened in that restaurant in Copenhagen. Where there had been a chasm, John had built a bridge.

Mikal Saahir

Mikal, the imam of an Indianapolis mosque, is a professional firefighter. A physically fit man in his late fifties or early sixties, Mikal is the most prominent and frequent Muslim attendee at the Wednesday luncheons. As one member of the group shared on a day when Mikal could not attend, Mikal is "the ultimate dream of what Chiara [Lubich] would have hoped would happen… He totally gets it."

Having come to understand his personal history, I was surprised that he would participate in an interfaith group with Christians. Mikal converted from Christianity to Islam. Given that many converts justify their change of heart by cataloguing the drawbacks of their earlier faith, he might easily have avoided re-engagement. Mikal does admit having had the proselytizing zeal of the convert when he first became a Muslim, but his reasons for joining the group reveal much about his character and spiritual maturity. "There's no card, there's no dues. So, what is it? It's to love everybody," he told me. That sole requirement of loving everyone, he acknowledges, is the hard part, much harder than paying dues and joining an organization. He pointed around the crowded deli and added, "To [love] that person over there, and over there, and over there, them too?" After a pause, he added, "Okay." On another occasion, Mikal explained his early attraction in the following way: When a Christian member of the group told him that the men sought to live the word of God, Mikal remembered thinking, "*Live* the word of God? That caught my attention." He had heard many Christians emphasize reading the word of God, but few Christians he knew seemed to live that word.

Over several lunches, Mikal expressed with great eloquence the place of interfaith in the Shapiro group. Developing relationships over nineteen years has never been about producing hybrid spiritual beings, a person half Muslim and half Christian. "We should remain as we are; otherwise it is not interfaith," Mikal stated. I learned from Mikal, as from the others, that Christians and Muslims come together not because they share a common understanding of God or revelation, and certainly not because they seek some mutually agreeable spiritual compromise. Rather, they share the call to live the will of God on a daily basis. Whether Muslim or Christian, each man understands that one vital aspect of living the will of God is to encourage one another in their spiritual lives. As John Welch said to Mikal over one of the lunches, "I have a great respect for you. How can I argue [against] your beliefs?" The goal is to see "the beauty of the other person, and when you recognize that, you recognize who it came from," John added.

For the group, what matters is the fruit of a person's life. Mikal explained that if the fruit is good, then God must be involved in their relationship. More than once, Mikal repeated his belief that "what we're doing here is the will of God." That belief is clearly shared by everyone around the table. Even five minutes with the group is enough to convince you that it has God's blessing.

Mikal, John, and others have known one another long enough to have navigated the darkness of 9/11 together. On several occasions, Mikal shared the reaction to that catastrophe among the Shapiro circle of spiritual friends. He recalled being at his firehouse that morning, watching the TV coverage and praying, "Please, don't let this be Muslims." Even before the identities of the perpetrators were known, his first instinct was to go to the mosque to make sure that it was intact, for there had been negative statements in the wake of the Oklahoma City bombing. Certainly, the numerous threatening messages on his answering machine made vandalism seem likely. "[However,] when the Focolare members heard about it, they called and said, 'We want to come and join you at your mosque on Friday.'" Mikal demurred because he did not want to place others in danger. Yet, he said, "Ten, twelve Focolare members came and joined us." Mikal's gratitude for that response is still fresh, as if this show of solidarity happened only days before. He spoke about how easy it is for Muslims and Christians, after hearing of a situation of risk and danger, to claim that they would have done the right thing had they had the chance. "So here are these members here," he said, nodding in the direction of John Welch and others around the table, "[who] had a chance to do a living example in a very, very difficult time, and they [did] it."

I came to appreciate Mikal's candor and good sense. I was especially impressed with his response when I asked him how American Muslims should act after the Boston Marathon bombing. Since 9/11, every terrorist attack attributed to Muslims seemed to require that prominent Muslim leaders schedule a press conference to repudiate the violence. I have watched those press conferences and heard those repeated statements of regret by Muslim leaders, even though many Christian friends ask me why those leaders don't speak out more about terrorism in the name of Islam. When I reply that Muslim leaders *do* speak out, they give me a look of disbelief. It seems that unless Muslim voices communicate their deep sorrow at the top of their lungs they will be accused of suspicious silence. I asked Mikal if he had felt this responsibility after Boston.

His response took my question in a somewhat different direction. "Muslims in general do what they always do; they try to distance themselves from the act and denounce it as they should do." He described that reaction, however, as "theatrical," as if Muslims "have to prove that they're good enough to be here in America." In a stronger voice he continued, "I'm not going to be an actor. I'm going to be real. I'm an American, I'm a Muslim, and I don't owe anyone any...display." To underscore his point, he shared a recent email. A woman from his mosque wrote that she "wasn't going to go through a bunch of hula hoops because...two knuckleheads [in Boston] who she doesn't know from a can of paint [and] who claim to have her religion [meant that she had] to do some extra steps to prove [herself] worthy of being in America."

To myself I thought, finally! Mikal was expressing what many American Muslims must feel after a terrorist attack when they face a double standard. After the shootout and fire at Waco and the bombing of the Oklahoma City federal building, both groups behind these horrific events claimed to be Christian-based. Yet, no Christian leaders had to distance themselves and their flock publicly from those far-right groups.

I could count on Mikal being a straight-talking spiritual friend. On the rare occasion when he could not attend the luncheon, the energy in the group dipped noticeably. Mikal is no token Muslim, and no one who ever spent a few minutes in his presence would confuse his humility with weakness. I was not surprised to learn that he is a frequent speaker at regional and national Focolare gatherings, nor that on seven occasions he has been invited to the Vatican.

Joe Masters

The third regular member of the Shapiro gang is Joe Masters, a pilot whose parents have been members of the Focolare in Chicago for over forty years.

Every group needs a member who can make acute observations as well as offer poignant criticisms. As Mikal is that person from the Muslim side, so Joe is that person from the Christian side. Towering over the rest of us (he stands 6 feet 8 inches), Joe can sit quietly through much of a lunch only to offer a pithy comment that brings us all to thoughtful silence. Joe is a realist, not a romantic, someone capable of speaking about numerous topics, be they Focolare matters, United States foreign policy, military history, or anachronistic airline regulations (Joe knows how many golf clubs a person could legally carry on a flight prior to and then after 9/11).

On several occasions, he shared how the weekly meetings had affected his life and his perceptions of global affairs. After commenting on the gulf between many American Muslims and Christians, he observed, "I've been coming here for five years, five years exactly… [Since coming here], hearing the word 'Muslim' doesn't set off the kind of alarm bells for me [that it does for others]. I hear the word 'Muslim' and I think of David Shaheed or Mikal Saahir." Some outsiders, especially Christians, find it difficult to understand the group's goal. They would ask the Christian participants, "Well, have you converted any of these [Muslim] guys yet?" To which Joe would respond, "The rule isn't to convert; the rule is to love." Joe offered the clearest explanation of Focolare's astonishingly inclusive approach to people of all faiths. "It's not so much to convert, to bring them into the fold," he said, "but to bring the Spirit to them, and let the Spirit bring us into community with each other."

David Shaheed

David Shaheed has been a Marion County Superior Court Judge for twenty years. Like Mikal, he was raised

Christian before converting to Islam. If I am ever put on trial, I hope to have this sensitive and soft-spoken man determining my fate.

Given David Shaheed's work, he is not always able to stay for the entire lunchtime conversation, but he stops by regularly. One week, John Welch waited until David left to tell me a story that illustrates what the group understands by doing the will of God in the present moment. In a case before him, Judge Shaheed recognized the three attorneys representing a defendant. In the past, before he was a judge, their firm had not paid David for legal services rendered. In sharing the story with the group, he admitted the temptation to punish them by making things rough on their client. Knowing that he would need to confess to his friends at Shapiro's what he had done, he caught himself. To do the will of God, Shaheed realized, was to give his fairest judgment to the young defendant. At the close of the story, John Welch caught my eye and said, "I am closer to David Shaheed than I am to my own brother. And I'm close to my brother."

David, like Mikal, exhibits no animosity toward his Christian upbringing. For him, David explained, Islam was "more like a completion. [Before] It always seemed like something was missing." Islam satisfied David's quest. "For me it was like, 'Oh, this is how it all fits together,' " he said. Converts often feel their lives suddenly making sense, but what David shared next surprised me. It was the most unexpected comment that I heard during my meetings with the group. "I actually feel more comfortable with Christians than I do with most Muslims." At first, I doubted that I had heard David correctly. Shapiro's can be a pretty noisy place. I asked him what he meant. "Well, so much of religion is also cultural, because [it is] where you were born that marks or determines what we are," he said. Had Jesus been born in the seventh century, David believes, he would have "been Muhammad." The reverse he thinks is also true. Had Muhammad been born in the first century, he would have "been Jesus."

Then, David trumped those first two surprising comments with a third. "For me, the example that I see in Christians is closer to Islam than the example that I see in [many] Muslims, if that makes sense. Christians are more naturally inclined to live the example of [Islam] as presented [in the Qur'an] than what I see in the Muslim world." This observation made me chuckle. As someone who has lived his entire life within Christian communities, I shared with David that I had made a similar observation, only in the opposite direction. While until recently my exposure to Muslims has been limited, I confessed that those whom I have met often seem quite Christ-like, by comparison putting me and other Christians to shame.

We sat in silence for a moment, bookends: two men about the same age, both named David, one Muslim, the other Christian. Looking back on his comments now, I circle them as the words that I wish every Muslim, every Christian could hear. Some Middle Eastern extremists endeavor to "cleanse" Syria and Iraq of all Christians, as well as of Shi'a, Yazidis, and Kurds. Some American extremists dream of a United States without Muslims, Jews, Buddhists, Hindus, and Sikhs.

What David Shaheed and I have experienced in spiritual friendship is quite common. In the life of the person of another religion, we often see reflected what is best in our own. While it may seem paradoxical, seeing in the life of person of another faith what is best in our own tradition is deeply moving; it encourages us to deepen our own commitment to doing God's will. If God is at work in this paradoxical way, we should consider persons of other faiths who enter our lives not as a problem but as a gift.

PART III:
OMAHA

THE FUTURE IS UPON US

I IMAGINE—PERHAPS IT IS A waking dream—meeting a leader of ISIS/ISIL. We do not know each other's language, so we cannot argue. Each of us is allowed to take the other to one place in the world that represents our hope for the world.

I wonder where the ISIL leader would take me. To a recently captured town, where everyone is living uniformly and traditionally? Or to a battlefield in Syria or Iraq strewn with the Shi'a, Syrian and Iraqi, Yazidi, and Kurdish corpses? In either case, the leader's unspoken message would be, "Here is the future of the Middle East and, by the will of God, the world."

Given the chance, I know where I would take my counterpart—to an unusual assortment of buildings in Omaha. Omaha? Yes, an antidote to religious extremism can be found in Omaha, Nebraska, and the following chapters will introduce the visionary leaders of this city's inspiring Tri-Faith Initiative.

The buildings that I am referring to are yet to be completed, but even their outline on a site map is inspiring. At the center will be situated a large facility. Multi-purpose in design, the Tri-Faith Center, along with an attached domed structure called "Abraham's Tent," will include an auditorium, meeting rooms, a coffee shop, space conducive to contemplative retreats, a digital research library and archives, offices for staff and research fellows, and a kitchen and dining facilities. As Tri-Faith Initiative's website states, the design of the building "reflect[s] our commitment to collaboration, connectedness, and community with our Abrahamic faith partners."

The most original feature of Abraham's Tent, which stands at the rear of the Tri-Faith Center, will be its flexible walls that can be raised like garage doors. Nancy Kirk, at the time of my visit Executive Director of the Tri-Faith Initiative, viewed this feature as a metaphor for the entire project. The tent of Abraham, biblical tradition holds, had sides open to people of all faiths, traditions, and nationalities.

From that central vantage point, the ISIS/ISIL leader would be able to gaze across the creek to the sixty-thousand-square foot Temple Israel, the structure that serves as a synagogue for the Reform Jewish community of the city. The lines of this building emphasize the horizontal, with windows looking west toward Abraham's Tent, the Tri-Faith Center, and the other two buildings.

Across the creek and to the north of the Tri-Faith Center and Abraham's Tent will be situated a third building, a mosque, which will be impressive for its simplicity of line. The mosque's proximity to Abraham's Tent and the synagogue will be bricks-and-mortar evidence of the "connectedness" referred to on the website. The final building on the property will lie south of Abraham's Tent and the Islamic Center, across the creek from Temple Israel. Here a church, a Christian presence, will complete the circle of Abrahamic religious centers.

The site that I have brought the ISIS/ISIL leader to see is not a far-off future vision. The land is there, gently rolling mounds that were once part of the only country club in this city open to Jews. Temple Israel is also there on the other side of Hell Creek, a stream that in the property's country club days was named for its penchant to gobble up golf balls.

The mosque, the church, the Tri-Faith Center and Abraham's Tent, however, were not yet constructed at the time of my visit. What did exist is a sign identifying the plot of ground where the mosque will be built—

as soon as possible, according to the chief rabbi from Temple Israel. Construction is to begin on the Christian structure in the near future.

Together, the four buildings represent the unfolding vision of the Initiative. The group's dream represents something rare in the world—three faith communities choosing to share space and orienting their worship facilities toward a common place of meeting. What the Initiative envisions can dismantle the great fear of all religious extremists— that close contact with persons of other faiths will weaken one's own faith commitment. More than a display of strength, ISIS/ISIL's "cleansing" of other religions in Syria and Iraq betrays fear of a religiously diverse world. The Initiative suggests how to dispel this fear. At the proposed site, each faith community will have its own space, so that they will worship separately. The Tri-Faith vision is not to amalgamate the different faiths. As Imam Mikal of Indianapolis so accurately observed, there cannot be "inter-faith" without the participants' devotion to their own faith traditions. Each participant in interfaith spiritual friendships is meant to be devoted to his or her own faith, but such devotedness does not invalidate the faith of others.

The architectural plans make clear that the Initiative honors the distinctiveness of the synagogue, mosque, and church while offering space and opportunity for cooperative interfaith events among the three traditions. Asking "Which feature of the plan is the more important —the three worship sites or the Tri-Faith Center and Abraham's Tent?" is the wrong question. Each aspect of the plan balances the other. The integrity of each faith tradition and the coming together of the three in cooperation and encouragement are equally important.

In December, 2013, walking the land where the Tri-Faith vision will one day be realized, I found it easy to imagine people, curious or devout, being drawn there, especially from places where religions are in conflict. Those rolling hills felt like sacred ground. I could imagine pilgrims of all faiths journeying here to commemorate and embrace the Tri-Faith vision of unity. I could imagine scholars taking sabbaticals here to study and propose new approaches to interfaith cooperation. I can imagine former extremists, even ISIS/ISIL members, retreating to this place for healing and reconciliation.

The Tri-Faith Initiative can provide part of the remedy for today's religious extremism. At other holy places around the world, however, the opposite feeling can be present. Often, the holier the site, the more fear and insecurity surround it.

For example, consider the Western, or Wailing, Wall in Jerusalem. Many years ago I visited this site, holy to three faiths. My memory of that visit is still vivid. No one who has been to the Wailing Wall can forget the fervor and sorrow that the site calls forth. Here at the holiest site in Judaism, an unadorned wall of massive stones laid in the time of King Herod, Jews pray and insert into the crevices small bits of folded or rolled paper on which they have written their petitions. Atop the Western Wall stand two mosques, the Dome of the Rock and the Al-Aqsa, the third holiest site in Islam after Mecca and Medina. There, Muslims remember the night journey of the Prophet Muhammad, this being the place from which he ascended into the heavenly world. A third holy site in this precinct of Jerusalem, mere blocks away from the Western Wall and the two mosques, is the Church of the Holy Sepulcher. Tradition says that this is the site of Jesus' crucifixion, burial, and resurrection.

Together, the Western Wall, the Dome of the Rock and the Al-Aqsa mosque, and the Church of the Holy Sepulcher cover a space comparable in size to the Tri-Faith acreage in Omaha. But Jerusalem does not contain an Abraham's Tent or a Heavenly Bridge. It is a great sorrow that unless there is a "tent of meeting" in Jerusalem, the Wall, the mosques, and the church will continue to orbit a darker center, one prone to tension, intolerance, and hatred. The name "Jerusalem" is associated with peace and wholeness, but at its core we find the broken shards of a fractured vessel.

Against the backdrop of Jerusalem, the brightness of the Omaha vision dazzles me with hope, a hope that the Tri-Faith experiment can be a beacon to Omaha, to the American Heartland, to the entire world. Perhaps I wish for too much. Or, perhaps, Omaha indeed witnesses to God's dream at this point in humanity's development. Other cities may follow Omaha's example and designate "tents of meeting" where people of diverse religious traditions can gather in peace and encouragement. At such sacred sites, through encounters that enrich the sacredness of those spaces, people of different faiths can realize that "sacred space" is God's space, is not "owned" by any one group.

The connection between the Omaha's Tri-Faith Initiative and the search for spiritual friendship should be obvious. In a sense, the Initiative is a concretization of that search. Both the Initiative itself and those who seek spiritual friendship are practicing something far more powerful than "tolerance." We tolerate a headache or a noisy infant on an airplane. In contrast Tri-Faith, by making spiritual friendship concrete, values the "other" as "neighbor."

Some might consider what I have described to be a hopeful utopian reality. Many have yet to encounter such a "utopia" (etymologically, a "no-place"). Nevertheless, for a few such as those I met at Shapiro's in Indianapolis and in the Tri-Faith Initiative in Omaha, the future is already here.

A WINNING RECIPE

From Ground Zero to Omaha

I MAY HAVE NEVER HEARD of the Tri-Faith Initiative had I not been embroiled in the 2010 controversy over a proposed mosque near Ground Zero in Manhattan. In an editorial for the *Indianapolis Star*, I argued that not only should there be a mosque near Ground Zero, but adjoining that space should be a church, a Hindu temple, a Jewish synagogue, a Sikh Gurdwara, and a Buddhist meditation center. I imagined a scene where a spectrum of worshippers and religious leaders, standing shoulder to shoulder, would bear common witness to the conviction that violence committed in the name of religious faith is a demonic distortion of religion's true purpose.

Given the politics of central Indiana, I should not have been surprised that my editorial created a stir. One typical response was, "Don't you know that Islam is bent on world conquest?" Of course, I also received appreciative responses from like-minded folk who loved the image of religious leaders standing together and witnessing to peace. Nevertheless, I believe my strongest supporters understood that I was sharing not a realistic prediction but a vision of a hoped-for future. However, the image of religious leaders standing shoulder to shoulder in some permanent witness stayed with me. I felt divine providence again at work when, a year later, I came across a newspaper article that described an interfaith effort in Omaha to build a synagogue, mosque, and church on a shared site. I felt a rush of joy and excitement that others were accomplishing what I had only dreamt about.

I asked Muslim and Christian friends in Indianapolis who are committed to interfaith if they had heard about the Omaha plan. No one had, but the concept intrigued them. I began planning to travel there, to see for myself what was happening and to interview the key persons involved. My first step was to contact Nancy Kirk, the executive director at the time, who graciously arranged for me to visit and conduct interviews in early December, 2013.

The fall semester ends in December and I am usually exhausted from grading the exams and papers that stand between me and Christmas break. That December I felt no exhaustion, drawing energy from those in Omaha who seemed to be living decades ahead of the rest of our country in terms of interfaith cooperation. My finals graded, I packed my interviewing equipment and began my journey to Nebraska. In past projects like this, I had come to value the time alone during long drives to think about the upcoming interviews.

But "time alone" may not be completely accurate. On more than one occasion other people join me, especially those I admire. In 2007, navigating the canyon roads of New Mexico, I happened to hear a Martin Luther King, Jr. sermon on the radio. For thirty minutes, it seemed that Dr. King was sitting in my passenger seat. On my trip to Omaha, somewhere in the middle of Iowa, I felt the conviction of two other interfaith leaders blessing my trip.

The first is Klaus Finzer, a philanthropist from Köln, Germany, who funded several of the most successful interfaith cooperation efforts in Indianapolis. His compassion matched by his generosity, Finzer believes that Indianapolis is positioned to become a key center for interfaith cooperation in North America. Once we met and I felt Finzer's passion for interfaith, I embraced his vision.

Although few recognize the name Klaus Finzer, even those involved in interfaith efforts, everyone has heard of His Holiness, the Dalai Lama. Few, however, know that like Klaus Finzer, the Dalai Lama is convinced that the American Midwest has a spiritual energy comparable to holy regions in Tibet and India. Feeling their blessing, how could I not feel that I was meant to take this trip?

Vision and Reality in Omaha

No complex of buildings, even those as impressive as the ones planned by the Tri-Faith Initiative, can overcome religious extremism. If buildings were enough, then Jerusalem, with the Western Wall, the Dome of the Rock and Al-Aqsa mosques, and the nearby Church of the Holy Sepulcher, would be the most peaceful place on earth. Instead, Jerusalem's most sacred ground is laced with religious hostility and the ever-present possibility of violence. By the Western Wall, guards stand ready to prevent Jewish extremists from storming the mosques on Temple Mount. At the Church of the Holy Sepulcher, levels of distrust and anger are so high that fights have broken out among the monks of the six churches that have rights to this site of Jesus' crucifixion and resurrection; in the past, the keys to the facility had to be entrusted to a Muslim.

While interfaith gathering places are important, the vibrant spiritual friendships that take place in those buildings will eventually overcome extremism. In Omaha, as in the Middle East, worshipping Jews will be able to look out of windows at a mosque and church nearby, worshipping Muslims will see a synagogue and church, and worshipping Christians will see a synagogue and mosque. And, unlike the tensions that commonly exist where these three faiths abut one another in the Middle East, Jewish, Muslim, and Christian worshippers in Omaha will derive hope and comfort from their nearness to one another.

Because at this point the Tri-Faith tract of land contains only the synagogue, one could conclude that Omaha has achieved only the first stage of its dream. But in terms of developing spiritual friendships among the three communities, the Tri-Faith dream is already being realized. The establishment and deepening of these friendships is the hope that Omaha offers to Egypt, Iraq, Syria, Lebanon, Nigeria, Israel, the West Bank and Gaza, the Central African Republic, France, Belgium, and other troubled areas of the world.

It is commonly accepted that increased globalization and cultural diversity are irreversible. In this coming world, religion either will trend toward extremism, such as ISIS/ISIL, or will move toward spiritual friendships. Religions will either build walls of separation or bridges of cooperation and encouragement.

The Right Time, the Right Place

When I asked "Why Omaha?" the best answer came from its people themselves. In interviews, members of the Tri-Faith Initiative expressed two convictions: one, Omaha had been chosen and prepared by God; and two, "The right people came together at the right time and in the right place." After my interviews I would add, "The right people came together at the right time and in the right place, and many of the right steps were taken in the very beginning."

"The driving force was the parking lot." So Dr. Syed Mohuiddin describes the germ of the idea that has become the plan of the Tri-Faith Initiative. For years, the reform synagogue in midtown Omaha shared a parking lot with the Methodist church across the street. Because the Jewish services took place on Friday evening through Saturday and Christian services on Sunday, the arrangement met the needs of both congregations. Sharing parking space led to other cooperative ventures between the two communities. But the Jewish congregation had grown and the community was given the generous gift of thirty acres in the fastest-growing part of Omaha, land that once belonged to the only country club of Omaha open to Jews.

That experience of cooperation between the synagogue and the church prompted Rabbi Azriel of Temple Israel to ask, "Whom do we want as neighbors in our new facility?" To the surprise of many and the delight of members in the Initiative, the rabbi suggested that the new neighbors should be the Muslim community of Omaha. "We got together. We met in the public library for our first meeting," Dr. Mohuiddin remembered. "And we all brought food." Dr. Mohuiddin then uttered the words I found so striking that I would return to them repeatedly in my interviews in Omaha: "There was instant trust." In my notes I underlined those words "instant trust" and added a question mark. Jews approaching Muslims to be their neighbors? Trust between these two communities? That is not happening in Jerusalem, or in other major cities of the United States. I felt that I had entered an alternative universe.

Dr. Mohuiddin shared more detail of that first encounter. "It was a wonderful meeting with an immediate sense that we understood each other; we belong together...The initial reaction was extremely positive. We didn't think...'What do these people really have in mind...Is there some hidden motive?' That thought never crossed my mind, and, I am sure, not in any of my fellow members.... I am not sure this could have happened without the will of God." I shared with Dr. Mohuiddin something he already knew, that since the State of Israel came into existence, the walls separating Jews and Muslims have risen so high that many assume it will take centuries to dismantle them. "While here in Omaha," I began. Dr. Mohuiddin finished the sentence: "It [took] a matter of a few years."

During my remaining interviews, I sought to have each person explain this unusual level of trust. Rabbi Azriel hinted that good relations between some Jews and Muslims had developed long before his community's offer to share land. "We had been visiting each other's homes for a long time, but this [sharing land] is a completely different aspect." Muhammad Javaid, a recent Pakistani immigrant, could understand my surprise at the Jewish-Muslim rapport. "This whole [Tri-Faith] project, I look at as...they are betting against all odds.... But once you meet the people, you start believing in this project."

Ultimately, it was D.C. "Woody" Bradford, a local attorney and one of the four original Episcopal representatives on the Tri-Faith board, who explained why Omaha is the right place for this interfaith innovation. "This didn't happen in Omaha by accident," he said. "Putting it simply, we basically believe in fairness. We've got what some people call a 'cowboy tradition.' You have to be a fair person here. We don't care really what your politics are, per se, even your religious attitudes and your religious perspectives, but you have to deal fairly with one another."

For Bradford, being a board member brings back childhood memories of the warm relationships between Jews and Christians, now with the Muslim community included in the conversation. "Everyone at that [initial] table when we sat down, regardless of whether they were Christian, Muslim, or Jew, knew that the other eleven were going to be fair.... Fairness in that context was to honor each other's opinion, and honor their religion, too. That's what people that are fair do. That [attitude] bound us together even before we sat down." Bradford helped me identify the bedrock that supported such amazing "instant trust." The grand buildings needed a foundation of essential trust, which suspicion and intolerance could have easily undermined.

The Right People, the Right Initial Decisions

The progress of the Tri-Faith Initiative might be ascribed to luck. But what members have accomplished and intend to accomplish is not due to mere luck. Dr. Mohuiddin attributes progress to "the will of God." Rabbi Azriel agrees. "I am a completely religious man, so I think that God just loved [the Tri-Faith Initiative concept]. There was something there that came from above." But the rabbi added a caveat. "I don't think that anything above can move if nothing moves down here, below." From the perspective of faith, Omaha shows what can happen when God's dream for peace is made actual through the courage and dedication of inspired and influential interfaith leaders.

I also saw God's blessing on Omaha during my first interview with leaders in Interplay, the interfaith children's program. I discovered that the director of the program was a recent seminary graduate whose studies focused on children's faith development within an interfaith setting. Where else in the United States would someone with this specialization be able to apply such a degree immediately? The uncanny fit between this person's gifts and Omaha's plan for an interfaith children's program is more than mere coincidence. Incidentally, it was the director of Interplay who, in my first set of interviews, described Omaha as "this hotbed of Abrahamic collusion."

The Right Ingredients

Innovative initiatives require three essential ingredients: vision, energy, and influence. Even those who disagree with ISIS/ISIL recognize that this Islamist group has surpassed others in the region because of these very characteristics. ISIS/ISIL's vision is clear: to remove Western influence from the Middle East, a region that has historically been colonized and carved up by Europe and the United States. The source of ISIS/ISIL's energy is also clear. Potential recruits see a chance to change history and, because ISIS/ISIL initially controlled productive oilfields, these fighters even earned a salary as part of the bargain. It is frighteningly impressive that no country has influence over ISIS/ISIL. Because they answer to themselves alone, they attract young recruits who are tired of Western-favored autocratic rulers and monarchies in the Middle East.

Those who would defeat ISIS/ISIL must expose its bankrupt vision, exhaust its energy, and deny its influence over disaffected Sunnis and other potential recruits. Airstrikes from a coalition of countries and ground campaigns have proved successful, but as is evident from increasing terror attacks in numerous countries, ISIS/ISIL cannot be dismantled except through a counter spiritual vision; a vision able to attract young people of the world who seek a life of meaning.

In the Tri-Faith Initiative a small group of people has all three of the essential characteristics shared by innovative initiatives: vision, energy, and influence. Here is ISIS/ISIL's Jungian shadow, a group who build bridges of cooperation and encouragement rather than walls of fear and hatred. Those who guide the movement share a vision, invest time and energy, and wield a positive influence on the wider community. Yet, as is true of most successful movements, everyone I interviewed agreed that Omaha has one charismatic leader with nearly Moses-like stature and energy: Rabbi Azriel of Temple Israel.

Rabbi Azriel

> "If you meet Rabbi Azriel,—there are lots of people who are 'hands' and 'feet' and even 'mind' of the Tri-Faith Center—he is the heart and soul. The enthusiasm he has is incomparable." *—Dr. Syed Mohuiddin*, leader of the Muslim community

Prior to meeting Rabbi Azriel, I had heard so much about him that I found myself excited and yet a bit intimidated. Nearly everyone with whom I spoke conveyed a "just wait till you meet him" attitude about this man.

Rabbi Azriel exhibits two particular Moses-like qualities. First, he has been the "leader of the leaders," the voice that both inspires and reins in other board members when they start drifting from their essential goals and values. Second, as was true of Moses, Azriel also has to care for and inspire those in Temple Israel who are wary of this new direction, especially of cooperating with Muslims. The rabbi is as impressive in reality as in legend. He speaks passionately and quickly but also listens hungrily to what the other person is trying to say. I sized him up quickly as a "verbal wrestler" —someone who grabs hold of a word or phrase and seeks to pin it down. Yet the longer we talked, the more I realized that in such wrestling, his goal is not winning, but desiring that hard truths be expressed.

The rabbi's origins are reflected in his accent. He was born in Israel and grew up surrounded by memories of the Holocaust. He says that he loves his homeland "with all my heart," but his background has affected him differently than others with a similar heritage. "Before I got to age twenty-three," he shared, "I had already buried some of my classmates from high school [from the Yom Kippur War]. So there is an open wound inside of me that needed to figure out a way of healing it, and I think that part of my commitment to Tri-Faith, to dialogue, and to the conversation...is some kind of a payback for my friends."

Those memories led to Azriel's vital role in bringing together the Jewish and Muslim communities. He still speaks with awe of the powerful connection that developed between these two often conflicting communities. "There was a complete leap, a complete leap. Something happened. It was as if we [got] to a place where we tried everything else and nothing worked and there [was] nothing to lose." Then, citing another parallel of his own to Moses, he connected what is happening in Omaha with the ancient Exodus experience. "I think God became a partner because of the cry that came from down here."

Three stories about Rabbi Azriel illustrate his critical leadership in Omaha; to both the synagogue community and the Tri-Faith Initiative. "When 9/11 happened," Dr. Mohuiddin recalled, "the first person to arrive at the mosque to guard the mosque was Rabbi. So that was the intensity of his concern for his fellow beings. Because there was no doubt that the mosque would be attacked, and he wanted to be there." The Omaha mosque indeed was attacked, as were many others in the wake of that cataclysmic event. Rabbi Azriel provided more details of what had occurred. "On September 11, I took members of this congregation to the mosque and surrounded the mosque on that day because I knew exactly what would happen—which happened, which was a lot of throwing stones, stopping the car, and cursing the people that were there. So we created some kind of a security belt around the mosque."

Months earlier in Indianapolis, I had been moved when I learned that on 9/11 the Catholic members of the Shapiro group had similarly stood guard at Imam Mikal's mosque. I was even more moved by what had happened in Omaha when Jews, some of whose relatives must have witnessed their synagogues being desecrated by the Nazis in World War II, guarded the mosque and even took verbal abuse for doing so.

A second story reveals Rabbi Azriel's courage. Under his leadership the Initiative's first order of business for was *not* to take the easy path of niceness but to confront the wounds that all parties carried within them. "I too cannot tolerate any more conversations on tolerance," he said. "I cannot tolerate conversations on dialogue... [or] the niceties of cups of tea or coffee and a cookie." Instead of a soft non-threatening approach that, he admits, "makes me sick," he proposed that the three faith communities say aloud what had to be said—meaning that all three religions must admit and deal with "harsh texts" that denigrate the other two religions. "So we have been doing in the last few years an...examination of harsh texts in our religious texts." In subsequent sessions with Jews, Muslims, and Christians, the rabbi explained, "I worked extremely hard with Muslims on the triangle of Sarah, Abraham, Hagar and Ishmael...You see, at different periods of time there was a harsh criticism of Abraham [in rabbinical texts] for kicking out Hagar and Ishmael to the desert. The Jewish commentators did not like his actions."

Rabbi Azriel led this courageous discussion by offering a high level of self-criticism. In examining the story of Abraham, Sarah and Isaac, Hagar and Ishmael, he considers it important to let Muslims and Christians know that some revered rabbis went even so far as "challenging God.... [The ancient rabbis were] uncomfortable with God doing what Sarah wants." After working through that seminal story of Abraham and his two sons, the group also studied New Testament texts that criticize Jewish authorities of the time and texts in the Qur'an that denigrate Judaism and/or Christianity. Outside the courageous context that the rabbi had created, this approach could be taken, perhaps, only in an academic setting where such a provocative course might be taught by a professor—as long as that professor had tenure.

I heard the third story about Rabbi Azriel from Nuzhat Mahmood, a young Muslim member of the Tri-Faith board. She smiled as she described his characteristic tendency to shake up the leaders of the Initiative. She asked me to imagine a board made up of highly successful attorneys, owners of real estate companies, and other civic leaders. Such meetings often begin with finances, but Rabbi Azriel "is one of the few people...who looks at the agenda and says, 'Now wait a minute. Look at his agenda. Is this our agenda?' He will look around and say, 'I mean, seriously. Is this our agenda?' Is this what we're about? Are we about budgets? No!' "

She laughed as she recalled something that happened at a recent board meeting. "He...would look at the building plans, at the roof, at the skylight, and he would say, 'Where is the soccer field?'... And we would all look at him, and he would say, 'I mean seriously, who cares about the building? Where is the soccer field where we can play? And where are the benches for a picnic? We're supposed to have a picnic.'"

On a more serious note, Nuzhat summed up Rabbi Azriel's gift of "refocusing on the essence of the heart." "The rabbi reminds us constantly that we are people and our person-to-person connections are [what are important]....He just seems to do this at the right time. His heart is truly full of love.... I don't know that anyone could fill those shoes with that much love and energy. He is unashamed. Rabbi is completely unashamed of upsetting the entire agenda."

As I prepared to meet Rabbi Azriel, nearly all of my other interviewees shared their sorrow that this gifted leader would soon be retiring. In our interview, when I told him of their sorrow, he was genuinely surprised and touched, but confirmed that he would indeed be moving out of the area. Many members will miss his guiding hand and caring heart. I could think of no greater compliment than this: every Muslim or Christian I met in the movement referred to him not as "Rabbi Azriel," but simply as "Rabbi." The rabbi of Temple Israel has also been Tri-Faith's rabbi, their teacher and mentor.

Dr. Syed Mohuiddin

A strong leader from one faith community, even one dedicated heart and soul to interfaith cooperation, cannot bring significant change unless other faith communities' leaders also come forward. For this reason, the Muslim community in Omaha is blessed to have the senior leadership of the noted cardiologist Dr. Syed Mohuiddin, and the youthful exuberance and energy of Nuzhat Mahmood. Despite the gap in their ages, both have offered wisdom and insight to the Tri-Faith Initiative.

Dr. Mohuiddin is a slight, soft-spoken man nearing retirement. His quiet graciousness complements Rabbi Azriel's forcefulness. Although subtle and understated, Dr. Mohuiddin's thoughtfulness and graciousness enhance the Initiative's effectiveness. Like Rabbi Azriel, Dr. Mohuiddin not only has offered to lead but also knows the right moment to do so. In 2006, after a progressive group headed by Dr. Mohuiddin regained leadership, the Muslim community realized their need for a larger mosque. "We knew that the Muslim community was growing. They were migrating mostly to the western part of Omaha. Therefore, we were thinking of buying a piece of land in West Omaha [to] build a mosque and teaching institute." During that period of self-examination, Dr. Mohuiddin recalled, Rabbi Azriel made his stunning offer. "And they [Jews], in thinking about neighbors to have on the new land, said 'Let's start with the Muslims.' "

Dr. Mohuiddin asked if I knew about the creek that bisects the property. I told him that I heard how the synagogue is situated on the east side of the so-called "Hell Creek," while the mosque will be on the west. Dr. Mohuiddin, however, wanted to share a different story. "People were telling us, 'you ought to change the name.' I said, 'No, let's leave it there.' And we will build heaven's bridge over it."

That image prompted my next question: What is your long-term dream for the Tri-Faith Initiative? He replied, "First thing, I think it would be an example for the people of Omaha and the state of Nebraska—and Iowa too—that people of three different faiths can live together peacefully.... They can agree to disagree on things, but they can resolve their disagreements peacefully, with some give and take on each other's part. [Omaha] is a neighborhood, and we want this neighborhood to be an example to the bigger neighborhood of the Midwest, and maybe even a bigger neighborhood which is the United States."

After a pause, he added, "If people could see that, I think we would have done our job."

I shared that the entire time I had been among Tri-Faith members, I kept thinking about the hostile scenes that I continue to see coming out of Jerusalem. The tiny area of the Western Wall and Temple Mount with its two mosques is occupied, but not shared, by the two religions. Those holy places, one literally on top of the other, remain a dangerous flashpoint.

"There seem to be a lot of Hell Creeks in the world today," I concluded sadly.

Dr. Mohuiddin nodded in agreement then added, "But not one heavenly bridge."

Nuzhat Mahmood

Nuzhat Mahmood's vivaciousness and enthusiasm complement Dr. Mohuiddin's quiet manner. Rabbi Azriel is the visionary; Dr. Hohuiddin is the respected influencer; Mahmood reflects the Initiative's energy. Her positive nature and ringing endorsement of the Initiative is all the more impressive because she knows that building this "heavenly bridge" has not been easy. Mahmood's story dispels the superficial assumption that Omaha has created a second Garden of Eden.

Bob Freeman, chair of the Tri-Faith board and a prominent member of the Jewish community, asked Mahmood to attend a lunch with members of the Jewish community who had expressed reservations about cooperating with Muslims. She was the only Muslim present. One of the group's initial questions she shared with me, was whether she affirmed Israel's right to exist. She recalled that some of those at the meeting wanted her to sign a written statement which began with this issue before other topics on the agenda could be addressed. What struck her immediately was that this is not what the Tri-Faith Initiative is about. "But for them, it was as if they did not want to talk to me until they knew where I stood on that."

In listening to Mahmood, I recognized a typical script: when two religious communities meet, it is common that the most contentious issues are pushed to the forefront. In the United States, some people view their faith communities as proxy lobbies for warring countries and communities in the Middle East and elsewhere. For many Jews and Muslims in America, global issues take priority over local realities. Her story raised an essential question: "Must such verbal battles always dominate the initial discussions between historically divided religious communities, or can the two communities meet one another first and foremost as neighbors in Omaha, Indianapolis, or Minneapolis?" "[The meeting] was exhausting," she recalled. "It is a lot of emotional work, where the stuff has nothing to do with you [personally]."

At the same lunch, Mahmood met another obstacle. Some Jews at the lunch forcefully maintained that dialogue with Muslims is not really possible. The meeting, she realized, quickly degenerated into a "one-sided airing of grievances." At that lunch she learned that interfaith relations cannot move forward until each person's story has been heard. "So there is an enormous amount of work [to be done], but then there's that patience that is [also needed].... I was happy to be that [person] to just sit, listen, to be fair, and to be non-judgmental."

Despite her calm silence, some of the Jews at the luncheon could not hide their contempt for her as a Muslim. She noted, however, other small gestures of openness, such as the husband of one very judgmental woman who shook her hand at the end of the luncheon and thanked her for being with them. Yes, a small gesture, Nuzhat admitted, but one that offered an opening for a future conversation that bridged their social and religious differences. Even in that contentious meeting something changed for the better in Omaha.

"I share this with you as a story just to say that it's hard work and not all fun and games," she said in conclusion. This reality, she suggested, is important to remember not only when the road turns bumpy, but also when events succeed and progress is made. Behind every step forward, she wanted me to understand, is a mountain of hard work. And, I thought, a mountain of patience.

D.C. "Woody" Bradford

> "All the Muslims that I have met... they're just like Nebraskans." —*Woody Bradford*

Not surprisingly, from the beginning progressive Christians have made a strong personal commitment to the Tri-Faith Initiative. In terms of drawing architectural plans and breaking ground, however, the Christian community lagged behind the Jewish and Muslim communities. The synagogue has already been built, while the Muslims are raising funds for their mosque. Only since my visit, however, has a Christian group committed to building on the site.

Theresa Newell, one of the Christian members, shared a partial explanation for the Christian presence being settled last. It can be easier to foster partnerships across faith lines than reach ecumenical agreement. Progressive Christians may find it easier to cooperate with like-minded Jews and Muslims than to create a unified front among the many Christian denominations in Omaha. She accurately noted that the denominations are so numerous and so different, especially in worship, that Christians committed to the Tri-Faith Initiative in Omaha worried about the possibility of "losing their [distinctive] languages" when an ecumenical Christian structure is finally built on the property.

This is not to minimize the strong Christian presence that has been on the board from the beginning. Woody Bradford explained that once the Christian community was represented on that board, the next order of business was for the faith communities to share their fears. Out of their varying concerns came a memorandum of understanding. "[Creating the memorandum] didn't take as long as one might think," Bradford clarified. Part of that agreement is the commitment not to proselytize one another. "It took us four or five meetings to come around to a memorandum of understanding that has never been amended."

Another early success for the Initiative was an interfaith dinner. "Dining under Abraham's Tent," which took place in 2009, was open to the wider Omaha community. At Omaha's convention center, three national faith leaders participated on stage in a public conversation. With young people from the three faith traditions serving as waiters, "the dinner drew about 1200 people. It was magnificent," Bradford recalled. "It captured the attention of so many people because it was such a positive event."

"We're still living in some of the glow of that [event], frankly," he admitted. "It was a huge splash." Returning to the topic of board meetings, Bradford emphasized how these meetings allowed each faith group to teach the others and learn from the others. He linked the Initiative's success to Omahans' inherent fairness, yet his excitement seems grounded in other factors as well. One of them is the leadership that emerged among the three participating faith communities. Bradford ascribes part of the group's success to the mixture of clergy and laity on the board. Clergy alone cannot bring about changes needed at the grass roots.

Reflecting on Bradford's assessment and my own experience with interfaith groups, I recalled that prominent leaders of faith communities often attend public events like Dining under Abraham's Tent or engage in sporadic, rather than ongoing conversations. Elsewhere in the United States, at academic conference settings or in meet-and-greet gatherings, faith leaders seem stalled in the initial phase of establishing significant relationships. In Omaha, however, faith leaders have been bringing together the right ingredients for some time. These close relationships have allowed the board, Bradford added, to communicate about "pretty tender things sometimes." Closely linked with stable and ongoing leadership, he suggests, is the transparency within the group. "Our communication has been terrific. That's why we're going to succeed."

The longer we talked over lunch, the more Bradford's enthusiasm grew and the more impressed I became with the entire Initiative. Although level-headed and aware of the obstacles involved, he nevertheless could barely contain his excitement about the future. "We have just begun the most exciting journey, not only in relationship to the Muslims and Jews, but in the Christian church here in Omaha. It's going to be dynamic; it's going to knock their socks off. People are going to be adjusting to something...even I don't understand," he admitted. "I don't even know where this is going. But I know it's going forward. I know it's going to happen."

Although Bradford's enthusiasm is understandable, such words might easily be dismissed if the Tri-Faith Initiative were just beginning with the members yet to face the storms ahead. But this is not the case in Omaha. Although obstacles still loom, the Initiative has already weathered, and is currently weathering, some serious threats to its existence, as we will see in the next chapter. The enthusiasm and confidence that I heard in all my interviews persist because members have been tested and not only have endured, but have kept moving forward. Progress may be slow, but it is steady. Omaha, with its Tri-Faith Initiative, is an epicenter of interfaith cooperation, a model not just for all of the United States but for the world. Anyone committed to interfaith progress can learn from the recipe being perfected there.

THE DANCE OF HOPE AND FEAR

Wherever hope flourishes, fear lurks in the shadows. I realized this dramatically in May, 2013, when I served on the planning group for the Dalai Lama's visit to Louisville, Kentucky. Because the Boston Marathon bombing had occurred just a couple of months previously, security came to overshadow all other issues. To ensure everyone's safety, Homeland Security and the FBI joined local police and security personnel at the venue.

For hours we stood in the hot sun outside the center where the Dalai Lama was to speak. Finally, one by one, we were allowed to pass through the elaborate screening process. The long wait culminated in additional hours in a secure room within the auditorium before we were escorted to our reserved seats—and we were part of the event staff! The irony of the moment was inescapable. We had come to hear one of the world's leading messengers of hope, of interfaith cooperation, of compassion, yet all was encircled by fear. As human beings, we were hungry for a message of hope and compassion, yet we could not be trusted because of our human tendencies for violence and hate. On that day, we needed to protect ourselves from ourselves.

The Threat from Outside: Going Undercover in Omaha

Hope and fear were present in Omaha, though not as dramatically as what I felt in Louisville. These emotions surfaced when I interviewed parents and children involved in one of Tri-Faith Initiative's most innovative aspects —the "Interplay" program. The website contains this description: "Interplay is a program for K-5 children and their parents. Together they learn about the Abrahamic faiths, and undertake community service projects. Registration is held in the summer for the following school year. If you are interested in enrolling your child, please send an email to…"

A bit brief for an advertisement, I initially thought, but I later realized that the brevity was intentional. My invitation to meet with those involved in Interplay came with several stipulations. I was asked to conceal the identity of the children in my writing, which also meant that I could not identify the parents by name. I was also asked to cooperate with the group's practice of not publicizing the location and time of the Interplay programs. While this can be standard procedure for the protection of children, I learned that there was more at play here.

Arriving a bit early for that evening's gathering of parents and children, I could feel something clandestine in the air. That morning, I was given directions to a nondescript assortment of offices where I would find a locked, windowless suite of rooms that had no signage identifying what would soon take place. As parents came with their children, I identified myself and explained my presence. The first child to arrive played video games while his mother and I chatted about the benefit of the Interplay program. As other parents and children showed up, I continued introducing myself while we waited for the parent with the key to the rooms to appear.

When that parent arrived bearing pizzas, we all entered the suite. After a brief tour of the three rooms, I took a seat in the first room with the parents and children. The children all knew one another and wanted what all children want—to play. They seemed a bit confused when their parents asked them to sit quietly for a few minutes and share their thoughts with me about Interplay. Not surprisingly, the change of routine and the expectation to share their experiences with a stranger with recording devices made the children a bit self-conscious and flustered. At any moment, I expected one of them to say, "Why don't you just watch us play together?"

Eventually, one of the Muslim pre-teens, in response to his parent's prompting question, spoke eloquently about learning through Interplay "to see [an issue] in their [other children's religious] point of view." This awareness in a person so young of taking multiple perspectives surprised me. At the college level we encourage such skills as part of a liberal arts education, and it is one of the most difficult to teach.

An enthusiastic cheer followed permission from one of the parents for the children to leave the room to play. I remained and waited to hear the parents' perceptions of the program. That morning, the leader of Interplay gave me several "heads-up." First, there would be no lesson that evening as she would not be there. The sole purpose of the evening gathering was to allow me to meet and talk with the children and parents. Second, she explained that Interplay had exceeded all expectations in one important regard. "Interplay has been a completely pineapple upside-down-cake kind of experiment. The kids have enjoyed it. For them, it's just additional friends," the leader said. Watching how these children were interacting with each other, I concurred with her perspective. The unexpected, "upside-down" part of the Interplay gatherings has been the program's effect on parents. For liability reasons, the leader explained, "You're not allowed to just drop off your kid." Being present and working together to prepare the food or assist in the lessons offered the parents the "opportunity to see all the things they hold dear lived out in actuality." The relationships that have developed between parents have been so rich, one Christian parent offered, that "the parents will go [to Interplay] whether the kids can make it or not."

I asked the parents about the reactions of their relatives and friends. A Muslim parent shared that his visiting father had been very impressed. A Jewish mother balanced that positive reception by adding that other parents in her faith community, although they knew of the Interplay program, had chosen not to join. Whether they made that decision because the group met in the evening or because they felt afraid, she could not say. "That was a little bit disappointing to me." A Muslim parent quickly agreed, citing a similar reaction from other Muslims. He had heard that there is a fear "that the kids will lose their identity" through the Interplay program. "Actually, I find it just the opposite," he quickly added. The more he and his children learn of other beliefs, the more they understand their own. "Learning promotes learning," he affirmed.

As an example of the interfaith curriculum's success, a Christian parent shared that her child had recently noted the similarity between the season Advent in his calendar and the month of Ramadan for his Muslim friends. Another parent reported that his child understood why a grocery store should not be offering special prices on ham for Hanukah! Religious sensitivity has also grown among the parents. One Muslim parent described becoming more respectful of Hindu employees at work. When ordering food for a company gathering, he had searched out a pizza parlor that when requested would make pizzas without cheese or eggs, which conscientious Hindus do not eat.

Facing Organized Fearmongers

The positive experience of both children and parents is offset by the resistance that Interplay has faced from theologically conservative churches and right-wing organizations. On Sunday evenings, Tri-Faith hosts a program for children and adults about interfaith relations. One of the Muslim parents mentioned a particular session when a speaker closed his talk with a YouTube excerpt showing Muslim children singing about the "five pillars," the main tenets of Islam. The next day a blogger from one right-wing group posted that Christians in Omaha had opened "their service with a Muslim prayer and with Christian people following [along]." The blog also claimed that Omaha children "were being indoctrinated with Islam within the Nebraska school system." To top off this misinformation, the blogger claimed that "the Tri-Faith community, supported by the Muslim Brotherhood, is being built in your city." Even though the parents I talked to considered the blogger's postings too ridiculous to warrant a response, they clearly smarted at the false accusations.

A Muslim mother recalled another discouraging experience, also following another of the Sunday evening sessions. "After our presentation at interfaith, we started talking, and the first thing he [a detractor] said was 'Muslims are taking over America,' and 'how can we let these guys do this?' " She added that his comment shocked the Christians and Jews into silence. Her husband broke in, speaking rapidly. "My daughter was there. This guy has no respect for children. Talk about a horror movie? This was a horror movie for me." "[These were] things that should not have been said in a church at all," a Christian mother agreed. "My twelve-year-old son heard some of the comments, and he was very offended and upset." She shared how her son wanted to yell at this person, which led to a teaching moment about the importance of non-violent, calm responses. "He completely does not understand how people cannot like Muslims," she said.

The same woman shared how bad she felt for one of the Muslims who had experienced this outburst. "So I sent him an email after and said 'I am so sorry.' It was like welcoming someone into your own house and they're insulted in your house." Her Muslim friend emailed back, writing, "Our friendship is the answer to this. Keep being my friend, and it's okay." At that moment, I thought of how this Muslim friend had summed up in the fewest words possible the hope for spiritual friendship. "Our friendship is the answer to this. Keep being my friend, and it's okay."

Perhaps, from another perspective, resistance from certain Christian groups could end up being a blessing in disguise. Yes, such anti-Muslim and anti-interfaith outbursts are intended to demoralize the members, and they have had some success. At breakfast that morning, one woman hinted that she feels burnt out by the struggle and is close to her breaking point. Yet slander and defamation can have the opposite effect, clarifying what is at stake in this battle of fear versus hope. Such attacks will lead many to strengthen their resolve in staying the course.

The Ongoing Wound of 9/11

In my separate meeting with parents at the Interplay program, I suggested that their children would likely become interfaith leaders in that future. I also shared that I envied them as parents, for they would see the impact of a program like Interplay on Omaha and beyond. Despite the rise of fundamentalism around the world, the demand for simple answers in an increasingly complex world, these children would grow to not only accept but also enjoy the religious diversity that will be commonplace in the future.

I related my own experience of working with college students, how once a mind is opened, it cannot be closed. "The culture won't be able to put the genie back in the bottle with your kids," I predicted. Yet, I also felt a responsibility to predict that their children would continue to battle religious intolerance as they grew older. I asked the parents to consider, as an example, what might surface in classroom discussions when 9/11 is taught. Unsurprisingly, these families had already faced this issue. "When my son's class talked about 9/11..." a Christian parent shared, "they talked about Islam. It was at that point that he [my son] realized that not all people accept Muslims. That's when he said, 'how can they think that? They must not know any.'" Introducing 9/11 had a noticeable effect on this group of parents. As I had found elsewhere in the country, for many the pain of that horrible event is still fresh, especially for Muslims.

One Muslim parent in the group clearly had mixed memories of 9/11. On one hand, in the wake of the disaster her family had experienced kindness, as they were invited to stay in other families' homes for protection. However, others had harassed her family by knocking on their door at midnight or by calling with threatening messages, demanding that they move out of the neighborhood. She also mentioned that women wearing the Muslim hijab had been attacked in the streets.

One story more than any other, however, revealed how fragile the situation remains for Muslims in Omaha. In the wake of 9/11, a Muslim woman known by some in the room had been overheard telling a friend that she would not take her children to the mall, as she had gleaned from the news that the terror alert level was high. Within hours, the police knocked on her door, questioning her. "Who tipped her off that there would be violence at the mall?" she was asked. "I watched what you guys told us on the news!" she tried to explain. The end result of this misunderstanding is that the woman's name remains on a flight list, meaning that she is detained whenever she travels.

The Threat from Within: The Persistence of Doubt

A far more powerful threat comes from influential members *within* the participating religious communities who, despite the official position taken by their community leaders, are not yet sold on the idea. In our interview, Dr. Mohuiddin hinted that building the mosque on the Tri-Faith site could not even have been proposed in 2006, when a more conservative group was in power. And, as several of the parents in the Interplay parents' group admitted, few other parents in their faith communities have expressed interest in joining.

Rabbi Azriel tells a story that offers the clearest example of the depth of doubt and fear in his community about a mosque being built so close to the synagogue. "A man comes to me early in the process—I would say about three or four years ago—and says to me, 'Rabbi, what are you going to do if a live hand grenade is going to be rolled in the aisle during services?' So, I have a sense of humor—you can't be a rabbi without a sense of humor—so I said, 'Oh, my God, so I will assume that someone in the congregation wants to kill me.' And then, I had to give him an answer. I said, 'There are two choices. One of them is that I will try to run as far as possible, but I am not good at running. I had polio when I was young. The other option is to fall on the grenade.' At that moment, the man stood up, the tears were rolling, and he hugged me. Later, he became a major contributor to [our] building here." Rabbi Azriel concluded with a smile. "It has been an interesting journey," he summed up. "People are people...I think change is hard.... Being able to erase the tapes playing in our hearts is certainly hard."

As are the other leaders I met, Rabbi Azriel is a realist. The leaders know that completing the synagogue, the mosque, the church, the Tri-Faith Center, and Abraham's Tent will be only the beginning. Even the "heavenly bridge" over Hell Creek will be only an initial step. Harder to bridge is the gulf between people's minds. For many, those bridges will come about gradually, first when Muslims leaving the Juma prayers on Friday drive past Jews coming into the same parking lot for Friday evening Shabbat services, or when Jews who are coming back on Sunday for educational purposes park next to Christians coming for worship. Perhaps when three faith communities worshipping in such close proximity becomes normal, the next step may occur, when Jews, Christians, and Muslims will wave as they pass one another. Finally, what may follow these friendly waves will be silent prayers for one another. That will be the day when the inner divisions begin to close up.

How the Tri-Faith Initiative Overcame International Tension

"[Something] happened in December [2009], and I didn't know if we'd have a Tri-Faith in January." Nancy Kirk, the Executive Director at the time, was describing the outbreak of violence in Gaza. I knew from past experience how tensions in the Mideast could scuttle interfaith efforts here in the United States. Years before, during a gathering of Christians committed to Middle East peace, Jewish and Muslim participants had agreed to participate in the discussions. Just days before the conference was to start, a violent incident in Israel produced two parallel outcomes. In the Middle East, peace talks between Israel and the Palestinian Authority broke down immediately. In America, the result was the same. The Jewish representatives also withdrew from a conference devoted to peace.

Perhaps, in the end, the biggest threat to interfaith progress in Omaha and elsewhere in the United States is not right-wing anti-Muslim or anti-interfaith groups or members of the Jewish, Christian, and Muslim communities who remain suspicious of one another. Threats to spiritual friendships in Omaha, Indianapolis, or elsewhere in the United States could come without warning from an ISIS/ISIL beheading on YouTube or a bombing in Israel, Gaza, the Central African Republic, France, Belgium, or Nigeria. Social media has made instant reporters of anyone with a smart phone, who can transmit their perspective on news anywhere, immediately. A Palestinian-American Muslim or American Jew in Omaha with a friend in Israel, the West Bank, or Gaza may be emotionally closer to a scene of violence in the Middle East than those in Israel or Gaza who live blocks away from the attack. The late Massachusetts congressman and Speaker of the House, Tip O'Neill, once said that "all politics is local." In our age, "all news is local."

However, the Tri-Faith Initiative of Omaha is still together, and how they survived the Israeli-Gaza crisis of 2009 offers a precedent for how they handled the renewed violence in Gaza in 2014 and how they will likely handle the brutality of extremist groups in the months and years ahead. During the 2009 crisis, Bob Freeman, the chair of the board and a member of Temple Israel, called an emergency meeting in response to the outbreak of violence in Gaza. Nancy Kirk remembered the tension in the room when Dr. Mohuiddin, the leader of the Muslim community of Omaha, rose to speak. Nancy and others present braced themselves, waiting for the shouting to begin, for both sides to blame the other, or even for the movement to die in those moments.

In a quiet voice, Dr. Mohuiddin offered the anxious audience one simple sentence: "My community is in great pain." Nancy Kirk compared the effect of these words to a dam breaking, as people saw the crisis not as a political issue, but a human one. "Everybody in the room was saying, 'What can we do? How can we make this less painful?' " Nancy remembered. Then Rabbi Azriel suggested, "Why don't we do a blood drive for Gaza?"

When someone pointed out that regulations would make it very difficult if not impossible to send blood overseas, three members—Rabbi Azriel, Tim Anderson, a Christian member, and Sharif, a Palestinian-American —"locked themselves in a room for three or four hours to come up with a joint statement on Israel-Gaza." As she retold the incident, Nancy began to cry softly and in a quivering voice, added, "[the joint statement] ends with 'How can we go on with Tri-Faith when there is war in the Middle East?' "

Tears streamed down her cheek as she paused before repeating the last words of the Tri-Faith joint statement. "If not now, when? If not us, who?" Those same words reappeared on the Tri-Faith website in the spring of 2014 when fighting erupted again in Gaza: "If not us, who?"

LIKE A BRIDGE OVER TROUBLED WATERS

What is God's dream for our moment in human history? How persons of faith answer this question, perhaps more than any other, will shape their response to the changing religious landscape of the Americas, Europe, and the world.

Some persons of faith find our "global village" so disorienting that they view our present time not as God's dream but as God's nightmare. They see a world so full of strife and hatred that God can do nothing better than end it. In apocalyptic texts that describe a world descending into confusion and evil before the final curtain falls, they see a script for our times.

Other persons of faith answer the question of God's purposes by assuming that nothing has really changed. In their view, God's dream is for all humanity to embrace one religious faith—theirs. Now, as did their forebears in centuries past, they believe that they have been called to convert the world. In their view, people of other faiths, no matter how devoted or devout, must be persuaded that the false path they are following will lead only to damnation. Such groups, of course, cite scriptural texts to justify this position.

Like many other people of faith, I am convinced that the world, though beset by deep-seated problems, is not ending, but changing. In our view, globalization and its interrelatedness are part of God's dream, a dream that the human race live in peace by loving our neighbors, whoever they may be. We, too, cite scriptural texts to justify our hope. This book cannot change the minds of those who espouse the first two positions. More effectively that anything I can write, the unfolding future will demonstrate how the world will carry on and how God's dream includes a diversity of beliefs. I hope that readers will consider the implications of God's dream that humankind live in peace. If this is God's dream, we will view our present age and its challenges differently.

One such implication is to reconsider Samuel Huntington's religious fault-line theory. In his book *Clash of Civilizations,* Huntington presents a map of the world with lines indicating the unstable borders between one civilization with a distinct religious heritage, such as the West, and another, such as those parts of the world influenced by Islam. Huntington argues that throughout history religious tension and violence have erupted along these fault lines. He concludes by suggesting that the future will continue the past; that is, we should expect more tension and violence along these same fault lines. But does Huntington's theory hold in light of God's dream of peace?

First, those of us involved in interfaith dialogue should admit that Huntington's theory of dangerous cultural and religious fault lines can be applied to circumstances beyond relations between nations or cultures. Fault lines also exist *within* countries growing more religiously diverse. That is, the suspicion with which some Jews, Christians, and Muslims view one another applies not just to Egypt, Lebanon, the Central African Republic, and Nigeria. Such fault lines can certainly be found in Cairo, Damascus, Jerusalem, but also in Murphysboro, Manhattan, and Indianapolis.

Second, by confronting Huntington's theory with God's dream of peace, we interfaith advocates realize that the problem Huntington describes needs to be renamed. From God's perspective, these religious fault lines are open wounds in the body of that divine dream of peace. Interpreting political and cultural fault lines as wounds in God's dream means that interfaith advocates can never accept Huntington's pessimism about the future. We do not believe that wounds will remain open. Rather, we believe that one day those wounds will heal and God's dream will become reality. So, by trying to see as God sees we hasten to prepare for that day.

Omaha, Omaha

During the 2013-2014 NFL season, a story circulated about the Denver Broncos quarterback Peyton Manning shouting "Omaha, Omaha," when he wished to change a play at the line of scrimmage. According to the story, the city of Omaha, which has no professional sports team, appreciated the attention this great athlete showed them. In a similar way, this book ends with the same call—"Omaha, Omaha"—as a signal to "change the play." Omaha is just that—a game changer.

On the morning of my departure I walked the property of the Tri-Faith Initiative. My visit to Omaha impressed upon me a particular image: a creek named Hell, during the rainy season a streambed of troubled waters, cuts through the property like one of Huntington's fault lines. On one side is the synagogue; on the other side will be a mosque and a church. That is what hell signifies—separated people, especially peoples of faith.

As Dr. Mohuiddin and Nancy Kirk explain so clearly, the problem that Hell Creek symbolizes is not resolved by renaming it. No, for those who love God, be they Jews, Muslims, Christians, Sikhs, Buddhists, Hindus, or others, the open divides between religions are truly hell. We can transcend the separations of our current hell by building Heavenly Bridges.

Spiritual friendships form that heavenly bridge. In spiritual friendships, partners do not remain divided by fault lines. In spiritual friendships, "grenades" of scriptural texts are not lobbed into each other's camp. In spiritual friendships, the partners do not seek God's peace through theological debate or theoretical speculation. Instead, each partner in a spiritual friendship prays for and assists in deepening the other partner's faith. The metaphor of "walking across a Heavenly Bridge" signifies such encouragement, such belief that the God who is loved in every religion wishes that we love one another in this simple yet profound, life-changing way.

At the end of one of my lunches with the Shapiro group, which has lived out their spiritual friendships for over nineteen years, John Welch left me with a final thought. Flashing one of his big smiles, he uttered what at first hearing seemed a very peculiar phrase. Only after I repeated the phrase to myself did I understand its beauty. That phrase is *Assalam Vobiscum*, an ingenious combining of the Arabic and Latin pleas for peace.

Was it just my imagination, or in that moment did I not hear the laughter of God's joy?

CONCLUSION: PERHAPS A MIRACLE

> Ask and it will be given to you; seek and you will find; knock and the door will be opened to you. (*Mt 7:7*)

> Take one step toward me [Allah], I will take ten steps toward you. Walk towards me, I will run towards you. (*Hadith Al-Bukhari*)

ON THE JOURNEY OF this book, I have taken a step toward Muslims with two hopes: one, that promulgating the concept of spiritual friendships will lessen religious suspicion and hostility in our country and the world; and two, that establishing spiritual friendships with my Muslim brothers and sisters will help me become a better Christian. I have been blessed throughout my journey, but the same questions that trouble any pilgrim dog me as well: "Have I taken this journey in vain?" and, "Have I missed the journey I was meant to take?"

Some readers may consider it a mistake to establish spiritual friendships between Christians and Muslims. Some might think I have taken a journey to nowhere because the fault line between Christianity and Islam can never be bridged. Some cannot come to believe that our post-9/11 world offers faithful Muslims and Christians a divine opportunity to span the fault line of that catastrophe by building bridges of understanding with one another.

I can sympathize with the conviction that there will always be tension between Islam and Christianity. Certainly, the mass media offers little evidence of religious understanding, cooperation, and spiritual encouragement between these two faith communities. Stories of religiously-inspired violence and fear abound throughout the West, Africa, and the Middle East.

Over the past fifteen years, especially during our world's darker moments, I too have doubted that interfaith spiritual friendships can lessen the religious intolerance and violence that haunts our world. In those moments, I have harbored a longing for some blessing, a hint that the journey I am taking is not in vain.

Am I looking for a miracle? I am expecting no miracle, at least in the sense of convincing proof. However, in the New Testament, miracles are considered "signs," and throughout this journey I have longed for that—a sign. Looking back over the past three years, I can identify many "signs" of hope. The rapport that Marwan and I established is such a sign. The warmth of friendship and support from the Shapiro gang is a sign of hope. I can imagine no crisis or misfortune that would destroy the love and care that these men have for one another. I take as a sign my unexpected rediscovery of Frank Laubach as a model and mentor. My seminary education of over forty years ago provided the equivalent of a phone book of names of theologians, saints, church leaders, and reformers. The reappearance just as I began this journey of Frank Laubach, whom I can recall being mentioned only once in those distant years, continues to fill me with awe and gratitude. Finally, the journey—no, pilgrimage—to Omaha with which this book concludes was filled with signs of hope and spiritual encouragement. Yes, I believe that signs of God's presence have led me on this journey.

Yet the most convincing sign of God's blessing on this journey has come in the form of what I call "spiritual synchronicity." By this I mean those unplanned, unexpected moments when a religious tradition other than my own has deepened my faith. I emphasize "unplanned," as these moments have usually occurred when I was not consciously working on this book project at all.

One such moment occurred on April 30, 2013, which that year corresponded with Tuesday of Holy Week in the Orthodox Christian calendar. Beginning with Palm Sunday, Holy Week services drew my attention repeatedly to the life-sized crucifix behind the altar. The crucifix is always conspicuously located there, but as Holy Week progressed I found my eyes and heart increasingly returning to that image. The Holy Week services portray Jesus walking toward the cross, and my mind and heart were moving toward the cross as well.

Holy Week in 2013 also occurred during one of the busiest times of my academic semester. While trying to keep my heart and mind in Jerusalem, walking the Via Dolorosa with Jesus, I still had classes to prepare and exams to grade. Consequently, on that Tuesday morning of Holy Week, I was frantically grading so that I could free my mind to attend the evening service undistracted. But sometimes, God intends us to be distracted. In the stack of student papers before me that morning, one addressed the topic of Judaism's key beliefs. The class was to have completed the assignment weeks earlier, but I had had to ask this particular student to resend it, as I had lost track of it. Those who have ever seen the desk of a college professor will understand. Consequently, this paper which I *should* have read weeks earlier providentially presented itself to me "out of time" on Holy Tuesday. The student included a quotation from Rabbi Harold Greenstein. "The Talmud teaches that 'In the place where a repentant sinner stands, even the righteous who have never sinned cannot stand.'" I marked the quotation in the margin, indicating that I found the observation a helpful contribution. Nevertheless, I quickly moved on to other papers and the rabbinic comment did not come to my conscious mind again.

In the Orthodox tradition, Tuesday of Holy Week is the last of three consecutive evening services centered on Christ, the coming Bridegroom. The three services are meant to prepare worshippers not only for Holy Friday and Easter/Pascha but also for the ultimate return of Christ. The scripture for the Tuesday evening Bridegroom service is always the story in Matthew's Gospel of the woman, understood as a fallen woman, who in gratitude for God's forgiveness anoints Jesus' head and feet with costly perfume. Orthodox liturgy highlights and appreciates paradoxes. In Matthew 26:6-16, the woman's act of thanksgiving is contrasted with the condemning attitude of the disciples, who consider the woman's gesture wasteful, and the reaction of Judas, who immediately after this scene goes to the Temple authorities to betray Jesus. This text leads to the beautiful Hymn of Kassiani, which is sung only once a year during Orthodox services. The Abbess Kassiani wrote this hymn in the voice of the sinful woman, forgiven by Christ, who bathed Jesus' feet with perfume and her tears.

By focusing on the paradox of two kisses, the service heightens the contrast between the attitudes of the forgiven woman and Judas. The woman's kiss of Jesus' feet reveals her overflowing gratitude and joy. The kiss that Judas will give Jesus two evenings later is a betrayal. The two kisses represent the two reactions of sinners to God's forgiveness: one of love, the other of condemnation and betrayal. As I heard the story of the forgiven woman chanted and then the Hymn of Kassiani sung, I felt the hairs on the back of my neck stand up as the Talmudic passage came flooding back into my mind. "In the place where a repentant sinner stands, even the righteous who have never sinned cannot stand." In that moment, in my heart as much as in my mind, text met text and I was cast headlong into a deeper understanding of the woman's joy. The rabbinic saying let me see that this woman stood "in the place where a repentant sinner stands, [where] even the righteous who have never sinned cannot stand." Together, the two texts shed light on the woman's joyful transformation as well as the self-righteousness that prevented Judas from knowing the mercy of God. The beautiful harmony of the two passages, one gospel and one rabbinic, overwhelmed me.

Later that evening at home, the joy that I had experienced in the service returned. I felt an irresistible urge to open my computer in the hope of finding a text in Islam that matched the uncanny conversation of the other two passages. Again, Providence led me immediately to a parallel passage in the sayings of the Prophet Muhammad, the Hadiths:

Sahih Muslim, Book 037, Number 6620

> Abu Sirma reported that when the time of the death of Abu Ayyub Ansari drew near, he said: I used to conceal from you a thing which I heard from Allah's Messenger (may peace be upon him) and I heard Allah's Messenger (may peace be upon him) as saying: Had you not committed sins, Allah would have brought into existence a creation that would have committed sin (and Allah) would have forgiven them.

As I read this passage, the three-fold harmony of the gospel story, the rabbinic saying, and the Hadith text on repentance and forgiveness washed over me. From the gospel account, I witnessed the woman's joy and abandonment of decorum as she was washed in the forgiveness of God. From the rabbinic passage, I was drawn into the woman's heart, in that moment when she stood in a most holy place forgiven, clean, and new before God. From the Islamic hadith, I was enveloped in even more light as I felt drawn into the heart of God, a God who loves nothing more than to forgive sinners. I was overwhelmed with wonder at what surely, I thought, was a sign. The threefold illumination radiating from these texts became a sure sign—to me—that my journey has been God-ordained and God-directed. Without spiritual friendships with Muslims, Jews, and other Christians, I would never have understood how a gospel story, a rabbinic saying, and an Islamic hadith were meant to come together as a key that opens the door into God's own heart.

When I speak about my experiences of spiritual friendships, I often share this story, this miracle, hoping that those who hear it will retell it to others who, in turn, will retell it to yet others. My hope is that one day extremists intent on violence in the name of religion will also hear this story. By God's grace, may this story and the stories of others who have entered spiritual friendships of encouragement melt their hearts. In the meantime, let these stories of God's love and mercy melt our own.

APPENDIX: WILL THE TRINITY EVER MAKE SENSE TO MUSLIMS?

> [I]t is important that Christian theologians should work out a doctrine of the Trinity which would not remain an arcane mystery known only to a few top theologians in an intellectual stratosphere, but which would be accessible to ordinary Christians. Ordinary Christians have to meet Muslims and members of other religions and have to explain to them how, although they believe that Jesus is divine, they believe that God is one.[24]

BECAUSE SPIRITUAL FRIENDSHIPS ARE intended to encourage one another not to debate theological differences but to deepen faith, none of my Muslim friends have ever challenged me to explain the Christian doctrine of the Trinity. Moreover, given that this book aims to focus on how spiritual friendships can lead to greater understanding and peace in the world, raising the issue of the Trinity might seem unnecessary.

Yet I share William Montgomery Watt's conviction that the Christian doctrine of the Trinity prevents Muslims and Jews from understanding Christians. If the Trinity is not to remain an "arcane mystery" that only a few Christian theologians can defend, then we Christians owe our Muslim and Jewish friends a clearer explanation of this doctrine.

What the Sufi Abdul Aziz raised in his correspondence with Thomas Merton in 1963 remains true: "[The question is] How to reconcile the belief in one God (tawhid) with the Doctrines of the Sonship and Trinity."[25]

As it did for Sufi Abdul-Aziz, the doctrine of the Trinity can impede conversation between thoughtful Muslims and Christians. It might be helpful if Christians had a way to explain how the Trinity does not violate the Oneness of God. Even if flawed, such attempts may contribute to a clearer understanding of the Trinity for non-Christians and Christians alike.

What follows may seem an unconventional approach to "describing" the Christian doctrine of the Trinity. Yet I hope a hypothetical question-and-answer conversation with a faithful Muslim might open up just a bit the inscrutable mystery concerning the Christian doctrine of the Trinity for my Muslim and Jewish friends. I also hope this approach is as fair to Muslims and Jews who are unfamiliar with the doctrine of the Trinity as it is to Christians who readily accept this belief. My objective is not to proselytize, but to help Muslims and Jews understand why their Christian friends can hold to such a belief and still consider themselves monotheistic.

"Is Oneness not the paramount truth about God?"

As a Christian, I agree. Yes, Oneness is the most important truth about God. That means that my belief in the Trinity cannot be some mental gymnastic, some "sleight of hand/sleight of mind" whereby I insist that I am "technically" a monotheist. If I as a Christian confess that God is "three in one," I must also confess that God is "One beyond the three."

"I do not see how you can reconcile your belief in the Trinity with monotheism, the Oneness of God."

That is a fair question, given that the doctrine of the Trinity may seem to advocate "tri-theism," the worship of three deities. Any Christian response to this query must begin by focusing not on the "three" but on what Christians understand to be the Oneness of God.

The doctrine of the Trinity will always be challenging, even for Christians, if taken to be a mathematical issue, a matter of numbers. A more promising approach to this doctrine is to focus on what creates oneness—divine love. But as divine love is too majestic and ineffable for the human mind to comprehend, a better starting point is to explore the opposite of oneness, which is brokenness or sin.

Judaism, Christianity, and Islam all agree that sin breaks apart relationships God intends us to have, be that relationship between humans and God, between one human and another (including the stranger), between humans and nature, or between a person and the person's own self. For all three religions sin is, by definition, an act or state of unrighteousness or "un-rightness," that which places us in wrong relations with God, neighbor, nature, and self.

"Can you give some examples of what you mean?"

Sad to say, examples of sin as brokenness can be found in every human context. As a professor, I have seen broken relations in various guises on the college campus. Stealing in a dormitory destroys the right relations based on trust that should exist in any shared living unit. Stealing also occurs at colleges and universities whenever a faculty member or student takes credit for the research or insights of another. That act destroys the commitment to honesty that is fundamental to the academy.

Sin as brokenness can also be seen in the context of the family whenever a child is abused or belittled. Those acts destroy the relations intended by God for family members.

In the context of society at large, brokenness is also evident whenever racism, homelessness, and poverty persist. These sins tear apart the relations that humans are meant to have with one another. And, as St. Paul wrote about the Church, factions warring within a religious community are a sin against that community's true destiny to be one, to be a unified body.

In the larger global context, the sin of war destroys the right relations meant to exist between two countries (think Israel and Palestine) or between factions within a country (think of the Syrian civil war). As a final example, I would cite the destruction of the environment as sin because it destroys the right relationship that humanity should have with nature.

To say that we live in a sinful world is to admit that we live in a world where the interrelatedness of all life is fundamentally damaged.

"But how is this understanding of sin related to God's Oneness?"

Muslims, Jews, and Christians agree that there can be no sin in God, for no sin can exist in the presence of perfect love. In asserting that, all three Abrahamic religions maintain that only love, God's love and ours, can heal the brokenness of our world. This is so because the nature of love is to unite, even as sin's nature is to divide, to separate, and to break apart. Put simply, broken relations are the result of sin; oneness is the result of love.

It is vital to note that this oneness-created-by-love is not a mathematical concept. Consider the biblical words found in many marriage ceremonies: "the two shall become one." These words do not mean that marriage destroys the individuality of either partner, but rather that in a healthy marriage there is a oneness of love, and in that love the true individuality of each partner is fulfilled.

And what is a harmonious, whole family but one in which love affirms and supports the individuality of each member?

Or consider what peace would look like on a global scale. As we can observe throughout history, peace is not attained through conquest. Peace is achieved when tribes, parties, and nations treat other tribes, parties, and nations with fairness and love, with the same treatment that they desire for themselves.

"I can agree that love creates a oneness in the human experience, but it is still not clear how human harmony is related to the Oneness of God."

So far, we agree that the world is broken by sin; we live in separation, sometimes hostile separation, from one another. But no matter how prevalent sin, brokenness, and separation are in the human experience, humans cannot accept this condition as normal. Despite our experiences to the contrary, we long to achieve peace by becoming one community, or, to use the Islamic term, one *Ummah*.

Yet, if this longing for oneness does not arise out of human experience, what is its source? Why do we seem to know inherently that seeking justice, offering mercy, and forgiveness are right actions while oppressing others is wrong? We humans cannot help but yearn for the healing of our brokenness, and that yearning comes from the ground of everything, the Oneness of God. The God who is One is all about making life one.

As a Christian, I express the Oneness of God in a slightly different way than do Muslims and Jews, though Jews and Muslims may disagree on the term "slightly." What I as a Christian understand through Jesus Christ is not only that God is love but that perfect love exists within God. God the Father, God the Son, and God the Holy Spirit are One, and have been eternally so, because of the perfect, unifying love that is the true nature of God.

For Christians, then, the Oneness of God is a *unified* Oneness based on perfect love. In this divine Oneness, the Father, Son, and Holy Spirit are so united by love that they never have acted, and never will act, independently of one another. In the love that lies at the center of the Trinity, Christians see both the antithesis of human brokenness and the cure for our human brokenness.

This has been the orthodox Christian understanding of the Trinity since at least the fourth century teachings of the Cappadocian Fathers—Basil, Gregory of Nyssa, and Gregory of Nazianzus. The love within God creates Oneness.

"Your explanation of the Oneness of God as a unified oneness achieved by love is new to me, but remains an explanation that as a Muslim I cannot accept. The Qur'an repeatedly proclaims that God has no son, no helper, and no partner. God/Allah is Creator and therefore is to be categorically differentiated from any created being, including Jesus, Peace be upon Him. Does my reaction disappoint you as a Christian?"

No, my goal is not to persuade Muslims and Jews to accept Trinitarian belief. Rather, my objective is to offer a way for my Muslim and Jewish friends to understand that, through the Trinity, Christians arrive at the truth of God's Oneness by a different route than they. We Christians do believe that we are monotheistic, but we can certainly understand how non-Christians may struggle with the Trinity. Even Christians, if honest, know the Trinity to be a *mystery,* though we believe it is a great mystery worthy of our adoration.

What I wish and pray for, as a Christian in spiritual friendships with Muslims and Jews, is that my Muslim and Jewish friends have gained a better understanding of how along with them I affirm that the only hope for humanity's survival and fulfillment lies in the unifying love of the One God.

Asalamu Aleikum. Shalom. Peace Be with You.

ACKNOWLEDGEMENTS

I am indebted to all who opened their hearts in these interviews, especially Marwan Wafa, the men and women in the Shapiro group, and the participants in the Tri-Faith Initiative of Omaha, Nebraska. To enter into spiritual friendships with you and to hear of your own experiences in spiritual friendships has changed my life.

I am also indebted to Kathy Carlson, friend, wife, and first editor of this book, for her constant support and sound advice. Thanks also to Sara Camilli, my literary agent, who has supported my writing projects through the years, to Tom Masters and Steven Cordiviola of New City Press, and to Stephen Camilli for their encouragement and helpful editing suggestions.

I will always be grateful for the encouragement and support of Franklin College, a wonderful learning community of colleagues and students. Finally, I am particularly indebted to students over the years in my Religion and Violence class who have asked the hard questions and shared their hopes of a more peaceful and just world.

ENDNOTES

1. Jessica Stern, *Terror in the Name of God: Why Religious Militants Kill* (NY: HarperCollins, 2003), 53-54.
2. Russell Shorto, "Keeping the Faith," *New York Times Magazine* (April 8, 2007): 43.
3. Edward Said, *Orientalism* (NY: Vintage Books, 1979), 38-39.
4. David Carlson, *Peace Be with You: Monastic Wisdom for a Terror-Filled World* (Nashville: Thomas Nelson, 2011), 99.
5. Ibid., 103.
6. Ibid., 113.
7. Frank Laubach, "Islam in the Philippines," *The Muslim World* (Jan., 1923): 57.
8. Frank Laubach, *Letters by a Modern Mystic* (Westwood, NJ: Fleming H. Revell Company, 1958), 10.
9. *Christian Spirituality*, edited by Frank Magill and Ian McGreal (San Francisco: Harper and Row, 1988), 516- 520.
10. Laubach, *Letters,* 29.
11. Ibid., 10.
12. Mahmoud M. Ayoub, "Toward an Islamic Christology," as found in William Montgomery Watt, Muslim-Christian Encounters: Perceptions and Misperceptions (NY: Routledge), 128.
13. Laubach, Letters, 21.
14. See also Sura 42:4-5.
15. Carlson, *Peace,* 158.
16. Ibid.
17. There is evidence that Isaac of Nineveh influenced early Sufi Muslims. See Margaret Smith, *The Way of the Mystics: The Early Christian Mystics and the Rise of the Sufis* (NY: Oxford University Press, 1978), 102.
18. Thomas Spidlik, *Drinking from the Holy Fountain: A Patristic Beveriary: Ancient Wisdom for Today's World* (Kalamazoo: Cistercian Publications, 1994), 359-60.
19. Laubach, *Letters,* 57.

20. Jim Gallagher, *A Woman's Work: Chiara Lubich: A Biography of the Focolare Movement and Its Founder* (NY: New City Press, 1998), 172.

21. "Wherever We Are in the World, We Are Together," *Living City* (May, 2012): 132-33.

22. Ibid.

23. "That Historic Day in Harlem: Q &A with Eli Folonari 15 Years after Chiara Lubich Addressed a Very Special Audience at the Malcolm Shabazz Mosque in New York," *Living City* (May, 2012): 10.

24. Watt, 147.

25. Sidney H. Griffith, "As One Spiritual Man to Another: The Merton-Abdul Aziz Correspondence," in *Merton and Sufism: The Untold Story: A Complete Compendium* (Louisville: Fons Vitae, 2005), 110.

New City Press of the Focolare

New City Press is one of more than 20 publishing houses sponsored by the Focolare, a movement founded by Chiara Lubich to help bring about the realization of Jesus' prayer: "That all may be one" (John 17:21). In view of that goal, New City Press publishes books and resources that enrich the lives of people and help all to strive toward the unity of the entire human family. We are a member of the Association of Catholic Publishers.

202 Comforter Blvd., Hyde Park, NY 12538
www.newcitypress.com

Further Reading

A dialogue of life: towards the encounter of Jews and Christians	978-88-6739-562-4	$14.95
Walking Together, Jews and Christians in Dialogue	978-88-6739-022-9	$19.95
Un dialogo para la vida	978-950-586-298-6	$22.00
Muslims Ask, Christians Answer	978-1-56548-430-6	$15.95
Living Dialogue	978-1-56548-326-2	$9.95
5 Steps to Living Christian Unity	978-1-56548-501-3	$4.95

Periodicals

Living City Magazine, www.livingcitymagazine.com

Scan to join our mailing list for discounts and promotions
or go to
www.newcitypress.com
and click on "join our email list."